ILLUSTRATED JUNIOR

SCIENCE

Dictionary

BY
DAVID GLOVER

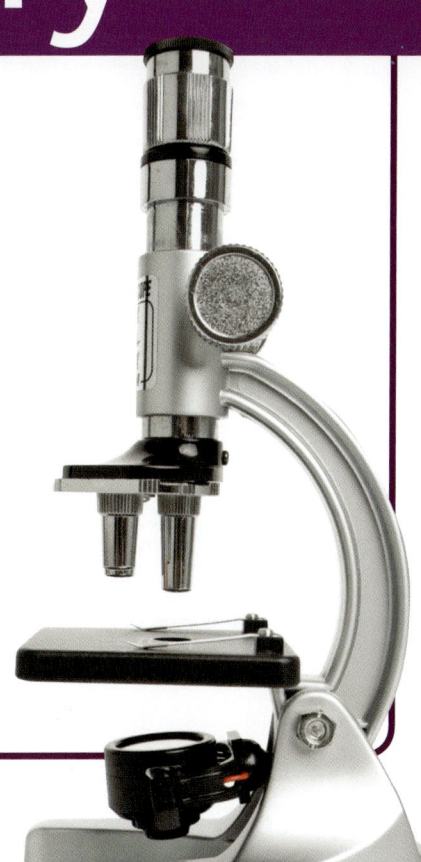

Published by Pearson Education Limited, Edinburgh Gate, Harlow, Essex, CM20 2JE.

www.pearsonschoolsandfecolleges.co.uk

Text © Pearson Education Limited 2011
Edited by Karin Fischer-Buder
Proofread by Elizabeth Barker
Designed and typeset by Scout Design
Original illustrations © Pearson Education Ltd 2011
Illustrated by TechType
Cover design by Scout Design
Picture research by Kevin Brown
Cover photo/*Front*: **iStockphoto:** Juliya Shumskaya (bc), Lisa Thornberg (tl);
Pearson Education Ltd: Digital Vision (frog); **Science Photo Library Ltd:** JPL / NASA (tr);
Back: **DK Images:** Alan Keohane (meteorite); **iStockphoto:** jsemeniuk br, Michał Strzelecki
(camera); **Science Photo Library Ltd:** (bl), NASA (cl); **Shutterstock.com:** Gilmanshin (eye).

First published 2011

15 14 13 12 11
IMP 10 9 8 7 6 5 4 3 2 1

British Library Cataloguing in Publication Data
A catalogue record for this book is available from the British Library

ISBN 978 0 435 07458 6

Printed in Spain by Graficas Estella

Acknowledgements
The author and publisher would like to thank the following individuals and organisations
for permission to reproduce photographs:

(Key: b-bottom; c-centre; l-left; r-right; t-top)

title page: **iStockphoto:** Juliya Shumskaya (bc), Lisa Thornberg (tl); **Pearson Education
Ltd:** Digital Vision (frog); **Science Photo Library Ltd:** JPL / NASA (tr); 2 **Fotolia.com:**
VIPDesign (b). **iStockphoto:** Heike Brauer (t). 3 **iStockphoto:** Lisa Thornberg (br). **Pearson
Education Ltd:** Digital Vision (bl). **Shutterstock.com:** auremar (tr). 4 **Pearson Education
Ltd:** Digital Vision (t). **Science Photo Library Ltd:** Andrew Lambert Photography (b). 5
Fotolia.com: Sascha Burkard (frog); outdoorsman (snake); Marilyn Barbone (hawk); Frank
Visler (wolf). **iStockphoto:** Jordan McCullough (butterfly). **Pearson Education Ltd:** Brand X
Pictures / Photo 24 (forest background). **Shutterstock.com:** Gertjan Hooijer (stork). 6 **DK
Images:** Andy Crawford and Tim Ridley (scales). **Fotolia.com:** ggw (burner); Andrei
Nekrassov (Galvanometer). **iStockphoto:** Massimo Merlini (weights); ginosphotos
(beaker). **Pearson Education Ltd:** Photodisc / C Squared Studios (thermometer). 7 **Fotolia.
com:** 2roxfox (t). **Getty Images:** D'arco Editori (br). **Science Photo Library Ltd:** Planetary
Visions Ltd (bl). 8 **Fotolia.com:** Eddie Toro (astronaut). **Pearson Education Ltd:** Photodisc /
StockTrek (tr). **Science Photo Library Ltd:** JPL / NASA (bl). 9 **DK Images:** Andy Crawford
and Tim Ridley (tr). **iStockphoto:** Henrik Jonsson (t). i **Fotolia.com:** Lasse Kristensen. 10
DK Images: Dave King (r). **Fotolia.com:** Poles (l). 11 **Alamy Images:** Medical-on-Line (tr).
Fotolia.com: Klaus Eppele (crow). **iStockphoto:** Roger Whiteway (heron); landbysea
(falcon); Jason Verschoor (background); Giuseppe Lancia (hen). **Pearson Education Ltd:**
Photodisc / Alan D. Carey (eagle); Imagestate / John Foxx Collection (owl). 12 **Fotolia.com:**
Duncan Noakes. 13 **Pearson Education Ltd:** Digital Vision (b, b/inset); Creatas (t). 14
Pearson Education Ltd: Imagestate / John Foxx Collection (bl). **Science Photo Library Ltd:**
Maximilian Stock Ltd (tr). 15 **iStockphoto:** rzelich. 16 **DK Images:** Clive Streeter. 17
Alamy Images: Myrleen Pearson (t). **DK Images:** Dave King (b). 18 **iStockphoto:**
Tommounsey. 19 **iStockphoto:** Sergii Tsololo (t). **Pearson Education Ltd:** Photodisc /
Photolink / J.Luke (bl). 20 **Fotolia.com:** a4stockphotos. 21 **Alamy Images:** imagebroker. 22
Alamy Images: Tetra Images (t). Science Photo Library Ltd (b). 23 **iStockphoto:** Piero
Malaer (b); fb1807016 (t). 24 **Fotolia.com:** jscalev (tr). Photolibrary.com: Robert Llewellyn
(l). 25 **Pearson Education Ltd:** Trevor Clifford (t); Photodisc. 26 **iStockphoto:** Rob

Broek. 27 **iStockphoto:** Carlos Gawronski (inset). **Pearson Education Ltd:** Image Source
(b). 29 **iStockphoto:** kyoshino. 30 **iStockphoto:** photovideostock (t); Björn Kindler (b). 31
Pearson Education Ltd: Silverpin Design Company Ltd (br). **Science Photo Library Ltd:**
Lixxie Harper (bl). 32 **Pearson Education Ltd:** Trevor Clifford (t); Photodisc / Photolink / S.
Meltzer (b). 33 **iStockphoto:** Robyn Mackenzie (cl); Richard Walters (t); byryo (cr). **Pearson
Education Ltd:** Photodisc (b). 34 **iStockphoto:** Tony Tremblay (b). **Pearson Education Ltd:**
Photodisc / Photolink / Kent Knudson (t). 35 **iStockphoto:** Christopher Futcher. 36
Pearson Education Ltd: Brand X Pictures / Burke Triolo Productions. 37 **Pearson
Education Ltd:** Imspace Systems Corporation (tl); Image Source (b). **Science Photo
Library Ltd:** Andrew Lambert Photography (r). 38 **iStockphoto:** ricardoazoury (sharks);
Grzegorz Choiᴆski (pink fish, striped fish). **Pearson Education Ltd:** Photodisc / Photolink
(bl); Imagestate / Ian Cartwright (grey fish). 39 **iStockphoto:** sugar0607 (l). **Pearson
Education Ltd:** National Geophysical Data Center (tr). 40 **Pearson Education Ltd:**
Photodisc / Jim Wehtje (l). 41 **iStockphoto:** Arpad Benedek (tl). **Pearson Education Ltd:**
Photos.com / Jupiterimages (bl); Photodisc / Russell Illig (br). 42 **Fotolia.com:** Lasse
Kristensen (l). **iStockphoto:** Mayumi Terao (r). 43 **iStockphoto:** Palenque. 44 **iStockphoto:**
Andrew Johnson. 45 **iStockphoto:** pierluigi meazzi (tr). **Pearson Education Ltd:** Imagestate
/ John Foxx Collection (tl). **Science Photo Library Ltd:** (c). 46 **Fotolia.com:** Jan Kupracz (r).
Pearson Education Ltd: Photodisc (l). 47 **Alamy Images:** David White (br). **Pearson
Education Ltd:** Trevor Clifford (bl); Digital Vision (t). 48 **Fotolia.com:** Sabine. 49
iStockphoto: Brian Balster (background). **Pearson Education Ltd:** Imagestate / John Foxx
Collection (bees); Digital Vision (ladybird); Creatas (br, red bug, black bug). 50
iStockphoto: Alasdair Thomson (tr). **Pearson Education Ltd:** Digital Vision (tl, tc).
Shutterstock.com: Konstantin Sutyagin (bl); Gilmanshin (br); Birute Vijeikiene (bc). 51
iStockphoto: Witold Ryka (t). **Pearson Education Ltd:** SNCF (b). 52 **Alamy Images:**
Roman Milert (br). **Fotolia.com:** DIA (tl). **iStockphoto:** Nancy Nehring (l); Juliya
Shumskaya (bc). **Science Photo Library Ltd:** GIPHOTOSTOCK (tr). 53 **iStockphoto:**
luchschen (tl). **Pearson Education Ltd:** Photodisc / Photolink (bl); Imagestate / John Foxx
Collection (br); Comstock Images (tl). 54 **DK Images:** (t). **iStockphoto:** Rob Sylvan (b). 55
DK Images: (b) Dave King (l). **Pearson Education Ltd:** Photodisc. 56 **Pearson Education
Ltd:** Nature Picture Library / Jeff Foott / Alamy (whale); Digital Vision (chimp); Digital
Stock (dingo); Corbis (giraffes). 57 **DK Images:** Steve Gorton (b). **Pearson Education Ltd:**
Trevor Clifford (tl). **Science Photo Library Ltd:** Planetary Visions Ltd (tr). 58 **DK Images:**
Alan Keohane (cr). **iStockphoto:** Tyler Boyes (b); Donall O Cleirigh (c); Andraž Cerar (cl).
Pearson Education Ltd: Photodisc / Photolink (t). 59 **iStockphoto:** jsemeniuk. 60 **Pearson
Education Ltd:** Digital Vision (bl). **Science Photo Library Ltd:** JPL / NASA (t). 61
iStockphoto: Tanuki Photography (bl). **Pearson Education Ltd:** Photodisc / C Squared
Studios / Tony Gable (br, bc). 62 **Alamy Images:** Westend61 GmbH. 63 **Fotolia.com:**
Sebastian Gorgol. 64 **Pearson Education Ltd:** Photodisc / Photolink / Jack Star (t); Corbis
(b). 65 **iStockphoto:** Michał Strzelecki (cr); Bob Ainsworth (t). Photolibrary.com: Corbis
(tl). **Shutterstock.com:** Stephen Firmender (b). 66 **Alamy Images:** blickwinkel (r). **DK
Images:** Clive Streeter (b). 67 **Pearson Education Ltd:** Image Source (bl). **Science Photo
Library Ltd:** NASA (tr). 68 **Fotolia.com:** Cosmin Manci. 69 **Science Photo Library Ltd:**
Power & Syred (t). **Shutterstock.com:** Heizel (r). 70 **Alamy Images:** B.A.E. Inc (bl). **Fotolia.
com:** Steve Byland (br). **iStockphoto:** SPrada (tr). 71 **iStockphoto:** narvikk (t); Mogens
Trolle (br). **Shutterstock.com:** Nola Rin (b); lsantilli (cr). 72 **Alamy Images:** DocCheck
Medical Services GmbH (cr). **iStockphoto:** FotografiaBasica (tr). **Science Photo Library
Ltd:** Sheila Terry (t). **Shutterstock.com:** MilanB (l). 73 **Alamy Images:** ICP (bl).
iStockphoto: eucylin (cr). **Shutterstock.com:** Joseph Dilag (tr). 74 **iStockphoto:** Debra
Wiseberg (t). **Pearson Education Ltd:** Digital Vision (b). 75 **Alamy Images:** Dave Pattinson
(tl). **DK Images:** Dave King (b). **Pearson Education Ltd:** Imagestate / John Foxx Collection
(cr). 76 **iStockphoto:** Ron Masessa (tl). **Pearson Education Ltd:** Digital Vision (snake,
tortoise). 77 **DK Images:** Albert Kerstna (b). 78 **iStockphoto:** Paul Morton
(br); JipJip.com (b). **Pearson Education Ltd:** Photodisc / C Squared Studios (bl). 80 **DK
Images.** 81 **Science Photo Library Ltd:** Charles D. Winters (b). 82 **Science Photo Library
Ltd:** Carol & Mike Werner / Visuals Unlimited (t). **Shutterstock.com:** Sergey B. Nikolaev
(cr). 83 **Alamy Images:** Barrie Harwood (br). **DK Images:** Ian O'Leary (bl). **iStockphoto:**
Viktar Malyshchyts (t). 84 **Science Photo Library Ltd:** NASA (b); Martyn F. Chillmaid (t).
85 **iStockphoto:** Marlee (r). **Pearson Education Ltd:** Photodisc (l). 86 **Alamy Images:**
Laszlo Podor (cr). **DK Images:** Geoff Brightling (b). **Pearson Education Ltd:** Photodisc (t).
87 **Shutterstock.com:** Sergey Peterman (br). 88 **Rex Features:** KeystoneUSA-ZUMA. 89
Pearson Education Ltd: Naki Kouyioumtzis (t). 90 **iStockphoto:** Paolo Florendo (l).
Pearson Education Ltd: Digital Vision (t). 91 **Alamy Images:** Scott Camazine (tl). 92
Alamy Images: Marvin Dembinsky Photo Associates (tr). **Pearson Education Ltd:** Trevor
Clifford (c); Photodisc / John A. Rizzo (tc); Brand X Pictures / Photo 24 (bc). 93 **Fotolia.
com:** Zsolt Biczó (l). **Pearson Education Ltd:** Fancy / Veer / Corbis (r)

All other images © Pearson Education

Introduction

Welcome to the new **Illustrated Junior Science Dictionary** from Pearson Education. We hope that you find it useful. The terms we have included are those you might need to use as you study science in primary or junior school.

Each entry has a similar structure as shown below:

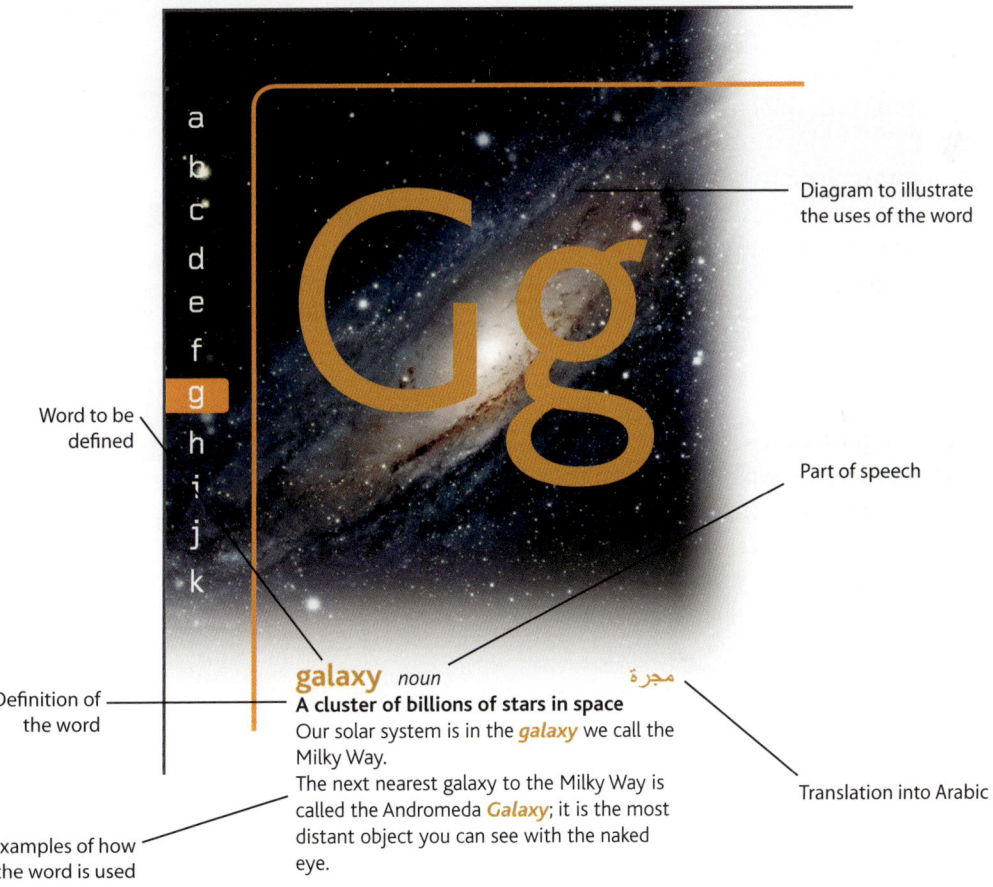

Diagram to illustrate the uses of the word

Word to be defined

Part of speech

Definition of the word

Examples of how the word is used

Translation into Arabic

galaxy *noun*   مجرة
A cluster of billions of stars in space
Our solar system is in the *galaxy* we call the Milky Way.
The next nearest galaxy to the Milky Way is called the Andromeda *Galaxy*; it is the most distant object you can see with the naked eye.

This dictionary is also available as a digital product on CD-ROM, if you prefer to use a newer way of checking the meanings of these words. The digital version also includes audio tracks (in British and American English) of all the words and definitions, along with word game, activities and simulations of some of the terms in the dictionary. It is quick and fun to use. To order the digital version contact your usual bookseller quoting the ISBN on the back cover of this book.

b
c
d
e
f
g
h
i
j
k
l
m
n
o
p
q
r
s
t
u
v
w
x
y
z

Aa

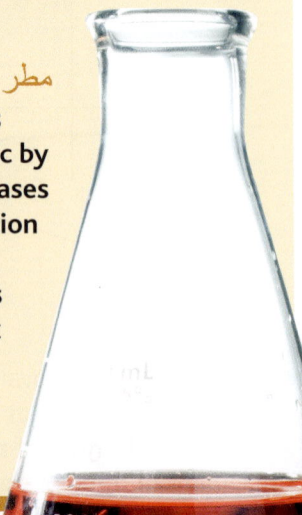

absorb *verb*   يَمْتَصّ

To take in or soak up

A plant's roots *absorb* minerals and water from the soil.

Dark surfaces *absorb* more heat radiation than white or shiny surfaces.

Paper soaks up water, it is an **absorbent** *(adjective)* material.

accelerate

verb   يَتَسارع

To speed up or get faster

The car driver pressed down on the pedal to make the car *accelerate*.

A force makes a mass *accelerate* in the direction of the force.

Adding fertiliser caused the plants' growth to *accelerate*.

accurate *adjective*   دقيق

Describes a measurement or observation that is carefully made and can be relied on as being correct

Rashid repeated his measurements to make certain they were *accurate*.

We used a digital stopwatch to measure the time *accurately* *(adverb)*.

acid *noun*   حِمض

A chemical that reacts with metals and bases to produces salts

Weak *acids*, such as vinegar and lemon juice, have a sour taste.

Car batteries contain a strong *acid* called sulphuric *acid.*

Strong *acids* are very dangerous; they react with human flesh.

acid rain

noun   مطر حِمضي

Rainfall that has been made acidic by pollution with gases from power station chimneys and vehicle exhausts

Trees and ancient buildings have been damaged by *acid rain*.

adult

adaptation   *noun*   تكيُّف

A special feature of a living thing that adapts it to its environment or way of life

Wings are an *adaptation* that enable animals to fly.

adapted   *verb*   تكيَّف / مُتكيِّف

How a living thing's body is suited to its environment or way of life; how a tool or invention has been changed to suit it to a purpose

Polar bears are *adapted* to survive in the arctic climate.

The inventor *adapted* the windmill to generate electricity.

adolescence   *noun*   مرحلة المراهقة

The human life stage between childhood and adulthood during which puberty takes place

Teenagers are *adolescents*.

During *adolescence* many young people experience changes in mood and feelings.

adult   *noun*   بالغ

The stage in the life cycle of a living thing when it is mature and can reproduce (have young)

An *adult* butterfly emerges from the chrysalis.

Some *adult* animals care for their young.

You will reach your *adult* height when you are 17 to 20 years old.

AIDS

AIDS
noun   الإيدز / مرض نقص المناعة المكتسبة
Acquired immune deficiency syndrome
People who suffer from *AIDS* lose the ability
to fight infection.
AIDS is caused by infection with HIV.

air   *noun*   هواء
**The mixture of gases that makes up the
Earth's atmosphere**
Nitrogen is the most common gas in the *air*.
Oxygen from the *air* is required for burning
and respiration.
Sound waves travel through the *air* from a
sound source.

air resistance   *noun*   مقاومة الهواء
**The force that opposes movement through
the air**
You can feel the force of *air resistance*
increase as your bicycle accelerates down
a hill.
The parachute uses the force of *air resistance*
to slow the skydiver's fall.

alkali   *noun*   قلوي
**A base that dissolves in
water; a base is a chemical
that reacts with an acid to
make it neutral**
The reaction between
the acid and the
alkali produced
a salt and water.
An *alkaline*
(*adjective*)
solution turns
red litmus
paper blue.

amphibian
noun   كائن برمائي
**A vertebrate animal that
lays its eggs in water but can
live on land as an adult**
Frogs, toads and newts are common
amphibians.

anchor   *verb*   يُثبِّت
To hold firmly in place
One function of a plant's roots is to *anchor*
the plant in the soil.

anemometer
noun   أنيمومتر / مقياس سرعة الرّيح
**A measuring instrument for recording
wind speed**
The *anemometer* showed that the wind
speed was 20 kilometres per hour.
The children made an *anemometer* with
spinning paper cups.

animal   *noun*   حيوان
(see opposite)

anther   *noun*   مِئبر
**The male part of a flower that makes
pollen**
Pollen brushes from the *anthers* onto the
bee.

animal

animal *noun* حيوان

A member of the Animal Kingdom of living things.

All animals have these characteristics:
- *animals* have complicated bodies made from many tiny cells
- *animals* obtain nutrition (their food) by eating other living things (mainly plants and other *animals*)
- *animals* have a nervous system that sends messages around the body

Tree and flowers are plants; worms, insects, goats and lions are *animals*. The plants are the producers in an ecosystem; the *animals* are the consumers.

Hawk

Snake

Stork

Butterfly

Wolf

Frog

apparatus

apparatus *noun*   أداة / جهاز

Equipment and measuring instruments for science investigations and experiments

Students should list the *apparatus* they need for their project.

Rashid studied the diagram of the *apparatus* for the experiment.

Put your *apparatus* away at the end of the lesson.

Weights

Ammeter

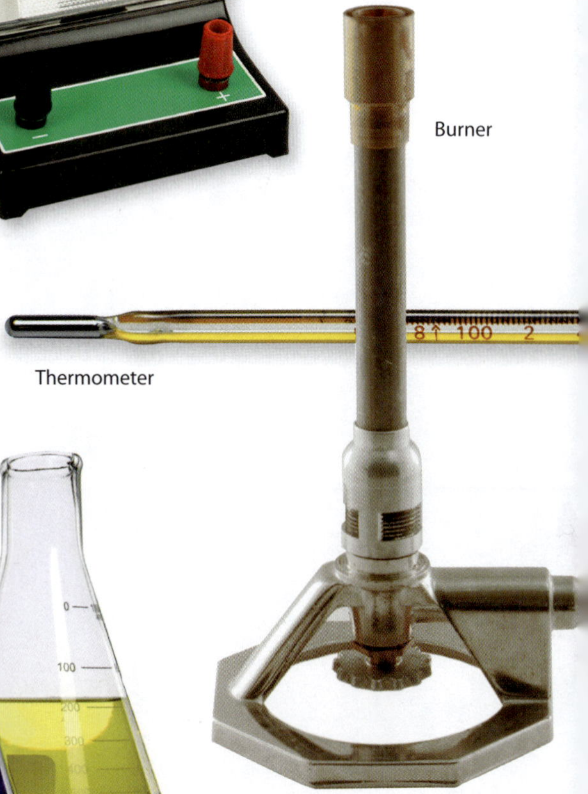

Burner

Scales

Thermometer

Beaker

artery *noun* شريان

A major blood vessel that carries blood from the heart to the rest of the body

The blood in an *artery* is rich in oxygen. Blood pressure is higher in *arteries* than in veins.

asteroid *noun* كويكب

A huge lump of rock in space; most asteroids in our solar system follow orbits around the Sun that lie between the orbits of Mars and Jupiter

One theory is that the extinction of the dinosaurs was caused by the collision of an *asteroid* with the Earth.

In future astronauts could mine *asteroids* for valuable metals.

arachnid *noun* عنكبوتي

An invertebrate animal with eight jointed legs

Spiders and scorpions are *arachnids*.

Arctic *noun* منطقة القطب الشمالي

The region of the Earth that surrounds the North Pole; the Arctic climate has low precipitation (rain and snowfall), short cool summers and long cold winters

The *Arctic* Ocean is almost completely covered by ice in winter.

The weather conditions were *arctic*.

astronaut

astronaut *noun* رائد فضاء
Someone who travels into space
Neil Armstrong was the first *astronaut*
to set foot on the Moon.
The International Space Station is
manned by *astronauts*.

atmosphere
noun الغلاف الجوي
**The layer of gas that
surrounds the Earth**
Heat from the Sun causes
water to evaporate from the
oceans into the *atmosphere*.
A barometer measures
atmospheric pressure.

atom *noun* الذَّرَّة
**The smallest unit (particle) that
makes up an element**
Each water molecule consists of one
oxygen *atom* and two hydrogen *atoms*.

attract *verb* يجذب
To pull towards or together
Magnets *attract* the metals iron and steel.
Unlike charges *attract*.
The force of gravity *attracts* objects with
mass towards the centre of the Earth.

axis *noun* مِحْوَر
**An imaginary line through the centre of
an object around which it spins**
The Earth turns on its *axis* once every
twenty-four hours.
The North Pole and the South Pole are the
opposite ends of the Earth's *axis*.

Bb

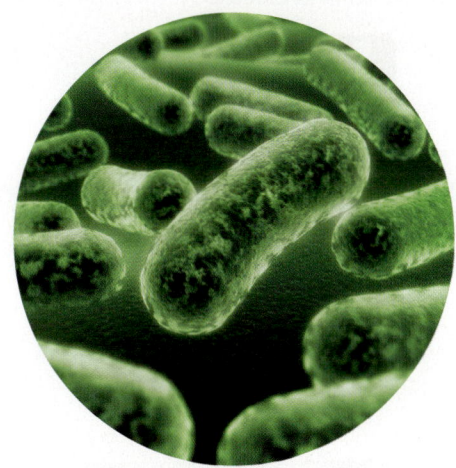

bacteria *plural noun* بكتيريا
Microscopic single-celled living things without a cell nucleus
Some *bacteria* cause disease, others help us digest food.
There are more *bacteria* in a handful of soil than there are people in the world.

balance *verb* يُوازن
To place or combine objects or forces so there is no movement or change
She *balanced* the book on her head.
The student moved the weight to *balance* the load on the lever.

balance *noun* توازُن
An instrument for measuring weight or mass
The shopkeeper weighed the apples on a *balance*.
A spring *balance* stretches to show the weight on a scale.

balanced diet
noun نِظام غِذائي مُتوازن
A diet that provides the correct quantities of all the different nutrients that the body needs for health
Fruit and vegetables are an important part of a *balanced diet*.
A *balanced diet* should not contain too much fat or sugar.

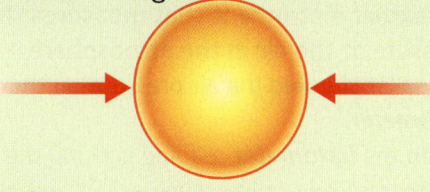

balanced forces
noun قوى متوازنة
Two or more forces that together produce no change in movement
Two *balanced forces* are equal in size but opposite in direction.
When *balanced forces* act on a stationary object it remains at rest.

barometer

battery *noun* بطارية

A device that produces electrical power from chemical reactions

The student connected the ***battery*** to light the lamp in the circuit.

A ***battery*** needs replacing or recharging when its chemical energy has all been transformed into electricity.

barometer

noun بارومتر / مقياس الضغط الجوي

A weather instrument that measures the pressure of the air in the atmosphere

The sailor checked the air pressure on the ***barometer***.

When the ***barometer*** reading is rising the weather is likely to improve.

base *noun* قاعدة

A chemical substance that reacts with an acid to make it neutral

Acid rain reacts with the ***base*** calcium carbonate in limestone.

A pH of greater than 7 indicates that a substance is a ***base***.

Big Bang theory

noun نظرية الانفجار الكبير

The theory that an enormous explosion of matter and energy created our Universe

Scientists estimate that the ***Big Bang*** took place 14 billion years ago.

Since the ***Big Bang***, the Universe has been expanding and cooling.

biodegradable

adjective   قابل للتحلل حيويًا

Describes waste materials that rot naturally

Vegetable waste is *biodegradable* but cans and glass bottles are not.
Biodegradable plant materials can be piled in a heap to make compost.

biome   *noun*   نظام بيئي حيوي

A major ecosystem such as a large lake, a major desert or a great forest

The plants and animals of a *biome* share the same climate.
The living things of a desert *biome* are adapted to survive in dry conditions.

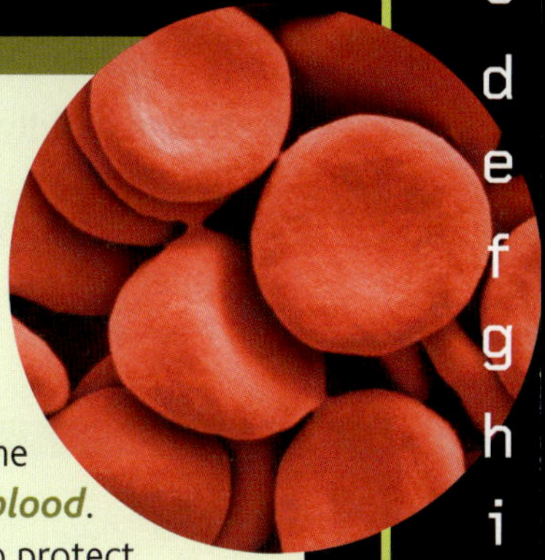

blood   *noun*   دم

The red liquid that flows around the body to transport oxygen, nutrients, waste and other substances

Following the accident, the patient had lost a lot of *blood*.
White *blood* cells help to protect the body from disease.

blood vessel   *noun*   وعاء دموي

A tube through which blood flows in the body

The heart pumps blood through the *blood vessels*.
Arteries are major *blood vessels* that carry oxygen-rich blood from the heart to body organs.

bird   *noun*   طائر

A vertebrate animal with warm blood and feathers; many birds can fly

All *birds* reproduce by laying eggs.
The ostrich is a flightless *bird*.

boil

boil *verb*   يغلي
To change rapidly from the liquid state to the gas state
He turned on the kettle to *boil* some water.
Salt water *boils* at a higher temperature than fresh water.

bond *noun*   رابطة
A join or a link between two things
The carbon atoms in diamonds are held together by strong *bonds*.
The *bonds* between the particles in a solid may be broken by heat.

bond *verb*   يربط
To stick together
Attractive forces cause the atoms to *bond* in pairs.
You can use a special glue to *bond* metal and glass.

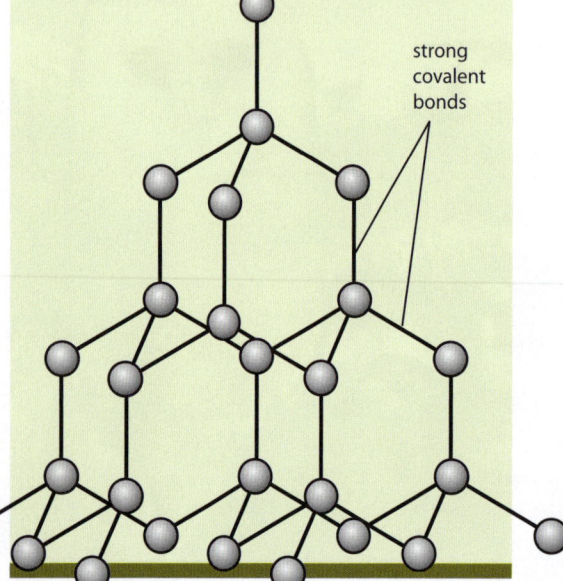

strong covalent bonds

bone *noun*   عظم
One of the individual parts of the skeleton of a vertebrate animal; the stiff substance from which bones are made
The femur, or thigh *bone*, is the largest bone in the human body.
There are more than 200 *bones* in a human skeleton.

burn *verb*   يحترق
To be on fire or glow very hot
The Sun *burns* brightly in the sky.
A candle *burns* with a yellow flame.

burning *noun*   احتراق
The rapid chemical reaction when a substance combines with oxygen, giving out heat and light
Melting can be reversed, but *burning* is a permanent change.
The disposal of waste by *burning* may produce air pollution.

buzzer *noun*   جرس كهربائي/ طنّان كهربائي
A small component that converts electrical energy into sound energy
The *buzzer* will sound when the circuit is complete.
The student uses a *buzzer* to make an alarm circuit.

Cc

Calorie *noun*   سُعْر حراري

A unit of energy often used to give the energy content of foods

An active teenager needs about 2000 *Calories* per day.

Cakes and fried foods have a high *Calorie* content.

camouflage *noun*   تمويه

Colours and patterns that make an animal difficult to see

The cheetah's spots are *camouflage*; they hide it from its prey.

Camouflage breaks up an animal's outline, making it merge with the background.

camouflage *verb*   يموِّه

To conceal or hide with colours and shapes

The moth's wing patterns *camouflage* it as it rests on the tree.

Wear green and brown clothing to *camouflage* yourself when bird watching in the woods.

carbohydrate

carbohydrate *noun* كربوهيدرات

The main nutrient in staple foods such as rice, cereals, pasta, bread and potatoes; sugar is also a carbohydrate

Most of our energy needs should be provided by eating *carbohydrate*-rich foods.

The complex *carbohydrates* in rice and cereals are healthier than the simple *carbohydrates* in sweet foods.

carbon dioxide
noun ثاني أكسيد الكربون

A non-flammable gas found in small quantities in the air

Plants require *carbon dioxide* for photosynthesis.

Burning fuel releases *carbon dioxide* into the air.

carnivore
noun لاحم/من آكلات اللحوم

An animal that mainly eats other animals

Lions and other members of the cat family are *carnivores*.

Carnivores are less common than herbivores.

carpel *noun* الكربلة

The female parts of a flower

The *carpel* has three parts – the ovary, the stigma and the style.

Pollen brushes from a bee onto the stigma at the top of the *carpel*.

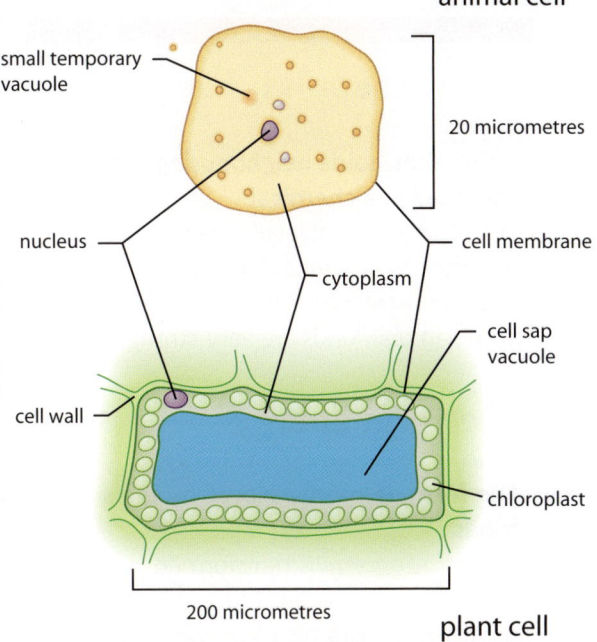

animal cell

small temporary vacuole

nucleus

cytoplasm

cell membrane

20 micrometres

cell sap vacuole

cell wall

chloroplast

200 micrometres

plant cell

cell division *noun* انقسام الخلية

The process by which cells reproduce by splitting in two

Damaged and old cells are replaced by *cell division*.

Through *cell division* the fertilised egg cell becomes two cells, then four, then eight, and so on.

cell membrane *noun* غشاء الخلية

The thin outer layer that surrounds a cell

The *cell membrane* holds the contents of the cell together.

Nutrients pass in through the *cell membrane*; waste materials pass out.

cell (biology) *noun* خليّة (أحياء)

The basic unit from which living things are built

The human body is built from more than 10 trillion *cells*.

Robert Hooke was the first scientist to identify *cells* under a microscope.

cell (electricity)

noun خليّة (كهرباء)

A device that converts chemical energy into electrical energy

A single *cell* has a positive electrode and a negative electrode separated by conducting chemicals.

Two or more *cells* are connected in series to make a battery.

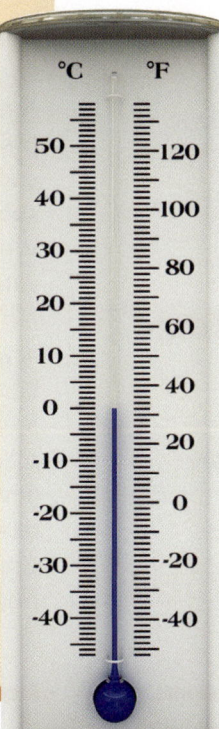

Celsius *noun* تدريج مئوي

A temperature scale and unit of measurement devised by Anders Celsius

Water freezes at zero degrees *Celsius* (0°C) and boils at 100°C. Because there are 100 degrees between the two fixed points, the *Celsius* scale is also known as the 'centigrade scale'.

CFC

noun مركب كلورو فلورو كربوني

A man-made chemical once used in aerosols and refrigerators

CFC is shorthand for chlorofluorocarbon.

CFCs released into the atmosphere have caused the hole in the ozone layer.

characteristic

characteristic *noun* خاصية

A special feature of a living or non-living thing

Small waxy leaves are a *characteristic* of plants that grow in dry places.

The student compared the hardness, colour and other *characteristics* of the rock samples.

chart *noun* جدول/مُخطط بياني

A table, graph or diagram for presenting data

Class Six presented the results of the litter survey on a bar *chart*.

The pie *chart* shows the proportions of the different materials that make up the Earth's crust.

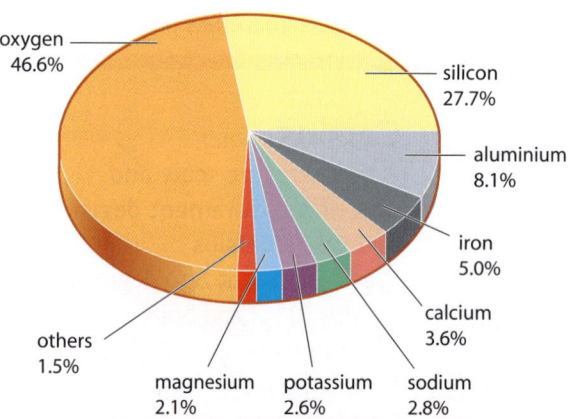

oxygen 46.6%
silicon 27.7%
aluminium 8.1%
iron 5.0%
calcium 3.6%
sodium 2.8%
potassium 2.6%
magnesium 2.1%
others 1.5%

chemical *noun* كيميائي

Any substance in which the atoms are combined in a particular way

A chemist is a scientist who investigates the properties and reactions of *chemicals*.

Acids, alkalis and salts are different types of *chemicals*.

chemical bond *noun* رابطة كيميائية

A link that holds neighbouring atoms together in a chemical

The atoms of a molecule are held together by *chemical bonds*.

The *chemical bonds* between the carbon atoms in diamonds are very strong.

chemical energy *noun* طاقة كيميائية

The form of energy stored by fuels and foods

Chemical energy is transformed into heat energy when substances burn.

A battery transforms *chemical energy* into electrical energy.

chemical reaction *noun* تفاعل كيميائي

A reaction that takes place when substances combine to make new substances

When an acid reacts with an alkali a *chemical reaction* takes place.

In a *chemical reaction*, bonds between atoms break and new bonds are made.

Some *chemical reactions* release energy as heat; others take heat energy from the surroundings.

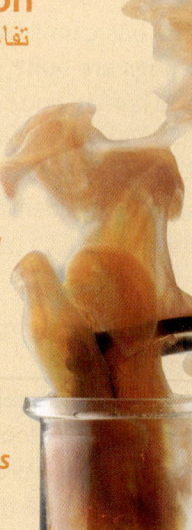

childhood *noun*   الطفولة

The life stage between infancy and puberty

During *childhood*, we attend school and learn to read and write.

Childhood should be a happy, carefree stage of life.

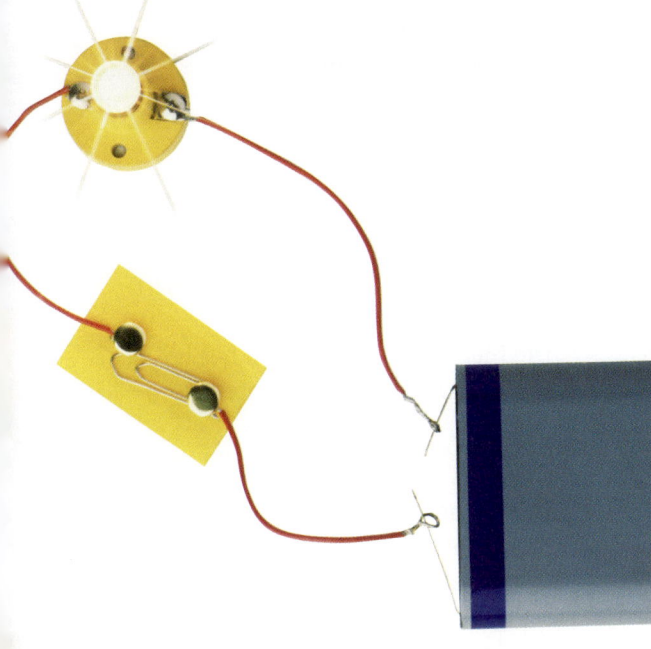

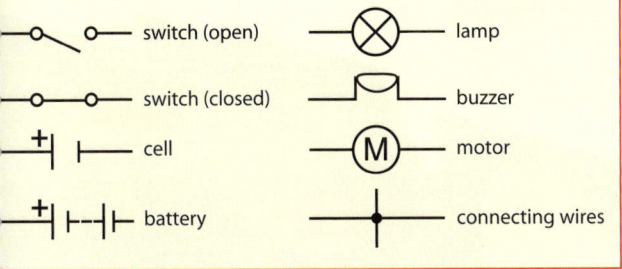

switch (open)		lamp	
switch (closed)		buzzer	
cell		motor	
battery		connecting wires	

circuit symbol

circuit *noun*   دائرة كهربائيّة

A complete loop of electrical components connected by wires, around which an electric current can flow

Rashid connected the battery, bulbs and wires to make an electric *circuit*.

The lamp did not light because there was a break in the *circuit*.

circuit component
noun   أحد مكونات الدائرة الكهربائيّة

Something that is connected in an electric circuit to perform a task or to transform energy

Light bulbs, motors, buzzers, switches and batteries are different *circuit components*.

In a series circuit the current flows through each *circuit component* in turn.

circuit diagram
noun   مخطط الدائرة الكهربائيّة

A plan of an electric circuit, in which the components are shown by symbols

The *circuit diagram* shows you how to connect the components.

If your circuit does not work, check the *circuit diagram* to see if you have wired it correctly.

circuit symbol
noun   رمز لأحد مكوّنات الدائرة

A symbol for an electric circuit component

circulation

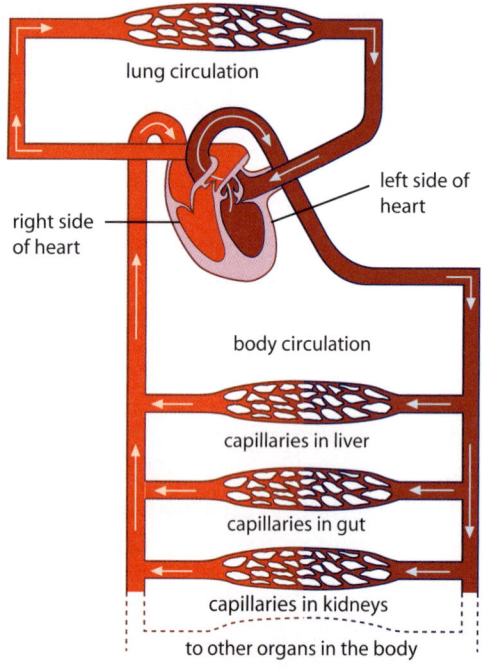

capillaries in the lungs

lung circulation

left side of heart

right side of heart

body circulation

capillaries in liver

capillaries in gut

capillaries in kidneys

to other organs in the body

circulation *noun* الدورة الدموية

The continuous movement of blood around the body

The *circulation* of the blood is driven by the regular pumping action of the heart.
When an animal dies its *circulation* stops.

circulatory system
noun الجهاز الدّوري (القلب والأوعية الدموية)

The heart and the system of blood vessels that circulate blood around the body

Oxygen, nutrients, waste and other substances are transported to and from all parts of the body by the *circulatory system*.
Regular exercise and a balanced diet help maintain a healthy *circulatory system*.

classification *noun* تصنيف

Organising living things, rocks or other items into groups according to their characteristics

There are five groups in the *classification* of vertebrates: mammals, birds, reptiles, amphibians and fish.
The species is the basic group in the *classification* of living things.

clay *noun* تربة طينيّة

A type of soil composed of very fine particles

Clay soils are smooth and sticky when wet, but bake hard when dry.
The *clay* soil sample retained most water.

climate *noun* مُناخ

The typical pattern of weather conditions in a region

Much of the Middle East has a desert *climate*.
The Mediterranean *climate* has hot dry summers and mild wet winters.

colour / color *noun* لون

The property of light, or a surface, that we see as red, green, blue or another shade

There are seven *colours* of the rainbow: red, orange, yellow, green, blue, indigo and violet.
A *colour* filter absorbs some light colours but transmits others.

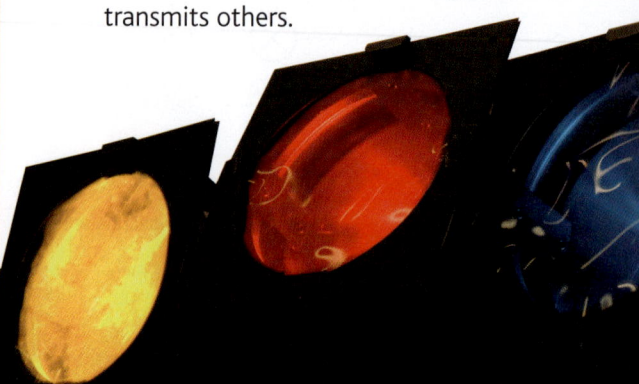

a b **c** d e f g h i j k l m n o p q r s t u v w x y z

comet *noun* مُذَنَّب
A large ball of ice and dust that travels around the Sun in a long narrow orbit
The orbit of Halley's *Comet* makes it visible from Earth once every 75–76 years.
As it comes close to the Sun, melting ice and dust particles give the *comet* a bright tail.

communicable
adjective مُعدي (مرض)
Describes a disease that can pass from one person to another, or from an animal to a person
Colds and flu are common *communicable* diseases.
Many *communicable* diseases can be prevented by good hygiene and by vaccinations.

communication *noun* تَواصُل
The process of exchanging information
The mobile telephone and the Internet are modern methods of high-speed *communication*.
The *communication* of observations and discoveries is an essential part of science.

compound *noun* مُركَّب
A substance in which the atoms of two or more elements are bonded together
Water is a *compound* of hydrogen and oxygen.
Oxygen is an element, but carbon dioxide is a *compound*.

concave *adjective* مُقَعَّر
Describes a curved surface that is hollow like the front surface of a spoon
A *concave* lens is thinner at the centre than at the edge.
A satellite dish has a *concave* surface.

conclusion

conclusion *noun*   استنتاج
The fact or facts you are able to state after considering the evidence from an investigation or experiment
The class discussed their *conclusions* at the end of the practical lesson.
The student listed her *conclusions* at the end of her laboratory report.

condense *verb*   يتكثف
To change state from a gas to a liquid
If you hold a cold metal spoon in the steam from a kettle, water will *condense* on its surface.
Cold drinks cans become wet on the outside because of *condensation* (noun).

condition *noun*   شرط/ظرف
A factor or state that may have an effect
Temperature, rainfall and other weather *conditions* affect living things.
In this experiment, you will investigate the *conditions* required for seeds to germinate.

conduction *noun*   توصيل
Heat transfer from particle to particle through a material; also the passage of electricity through a material
Heat travels through the base of a cooking pot by *conduction*.
A break in a circuit prevents the *conduction* of electricity through the components.

conductor *noun*   مُوَصِّل
A material through which electricity flows readily; a material that conducts heat well
A car radiator should be made from a good heat *conductor*.
The metal silver is the best *conductor* of electricity at normal temperatures.

conservation of energy

conservation

noun   حفظ / بقاء

The process of protecting something so that it is not harmed, changed or used up

The *conservation* of rain forests and coral reefs protects endangered species.
Conservation projects aim to save the tiger and other rare animals.

conservation of energy

noun   قانون حفظ (بقاء) الطاقة

The principle that energy cannot be created or destroyed, only converted to other forms

The principle of the *conservation of energy* tells us that the energy output from any machine cannot be greater than the energy input.

The scientist used the principle of the *conservation of energy* to show that perpetual motion is impossible.

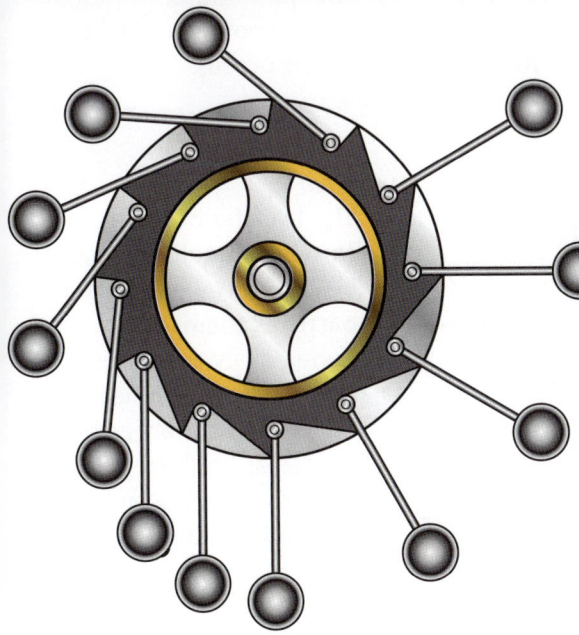

The principle of the *conservation of energy* tells us that, no matter how clever, designs for perpetual motion machines can never work in practice.

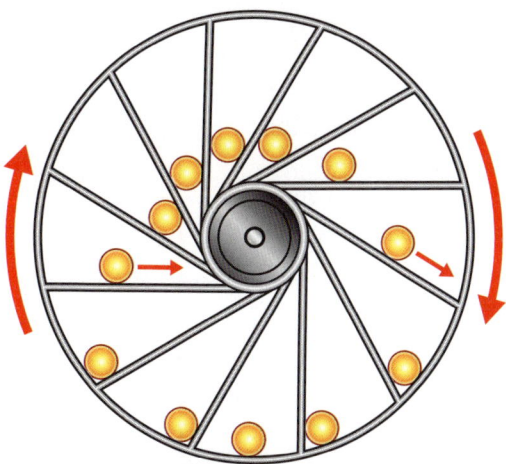

consumer

consumer *noun* مستهلك
A living thing that obtains its energy by eating producers (plants)
The plants in a food chain are the producers; the animals are the *consumers*.
Rabbits and other herbivores are primary *consumers*; an animal that eats herbivores is a secondary *consumer*.

contact force
noun قوى التلامس
The pushing force between two things when they touch
When a bat strikes a ball the *contact force* changes the ball's speed and direction.
The *contact force* of the floor on your feet balances the force of gravity pulling your body down.

contagious *adjective* (بالتلامس) مُعدي
Describes a disease or infection that spreads from person to person by direct or indirect touch (touching contaminated objects)
Regular hand washing helps prevent the spread of *contagious* diseases.
Head lice are *contagious* parasites that often spread in schools.

continental climate *noun* مناخ قاري
A climate with hot dry summers and freezing winters, often with heavy snow
Regions of large land masses far from the coast have a *continental climate*.
A *continental climate* is not influenced by winds blowing from the oceans.

convection *noun* حَمْل حراري
The transfer of heat through a liquid or a gas by the movement of the particles themselves
Currents of warm air rise from a *convection* heater.
Convection currents are created as hot fluid expands and rises and cool fluid sinks to takes its place.

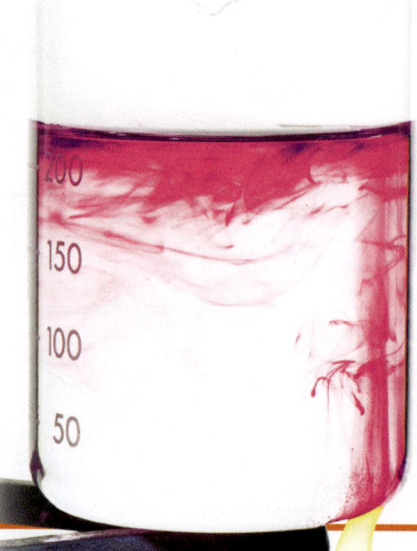

cornea

core *noun*　　　　　　قلب / لب
The centre of the Earth; also the material at the centre of the Earth
The Earth's *core* is composed of the metals iron and nickel.
The outer layer of the *core* is molten; the inner layer is solid.

cornea *noun*　　　　　　قرنية
The strong transparent protective covering that forms the outer surface of the eye
Light rays bend as they enter the *cornea*.
The surface of the *cornea* is kept moist by a film of tears.

convex *adjective*　　　　　　مُحدَّب
Describes a curved surface that bulges like the back surface of a spoon
A *convex* lens is thicker at the centre than at the edge.
The security mirror in a shop has a *convex* surface.

cool *verb*　　　　　　يبرد
To reduce in temperature or take away heat
Cool the specimens by placing them in a refrigerator.
As the Universe expands from the Big Bang it *cools*.

coral reef *noun*　　　　شعاب مرجانية
A large underwater rocky structure formed by communities of invertebrate animals called polyps
A *coral reef* provides a habitat for a wide variety of colourful fish species.
Coral reefs are amongst the most varied marine ecosystems.

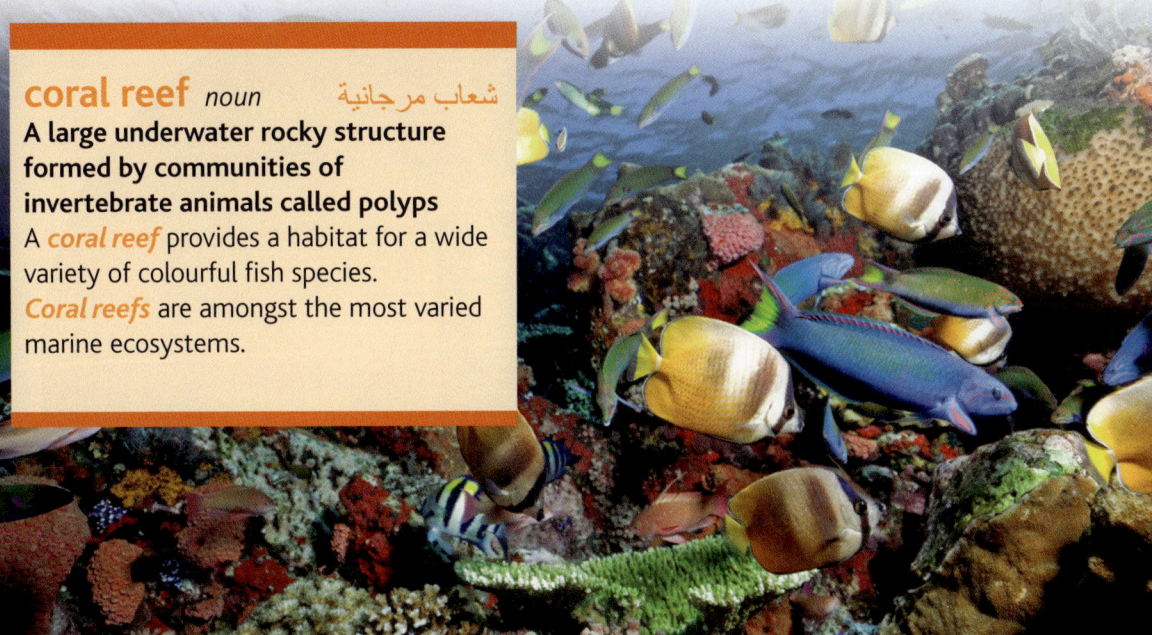

crater

crater
noun فوهة / حفرة صغيرة ذات حافة مرتفعة
A roughly circular, dish-shaped hole
The Moon's surface is covered with *craters*.
Meteor *Crater* in Arizona was formed
by the impact of a meteorite weighing
300 000 tonnes.

crust *noun* قشرة خارجية
The solid outer layer of the Earth
The Earth's *crust* is made from
igneous, metamorphic and
sedimentary rocks.
The continental *crust* is 30–50
km thick; the oceanic crust is
5–10 km thick.

crustacean
noun حيوان مائي من القشريات
An invertebrate animal with a hard outer skeleton and a body divided into segments; most crustaceans live in water
Shrimps, crabs and lobsters are *crustaceans*.
Crustaceans have been called 'the insects of the sea'.

current *noun* تيار
A flow of something – water or electric charge for example
The battery is the source of the electric *current* in the circuit.
A *current* of warm air rises from the candle flame.

solid outer crust
solid mantle
solid inner core
radius = 6400 km
liquid outer core

Dd

data *plural noun*
بيانات

Information; the results of measurements, observations and surveys recorded as facts and/or figures

The students planned to collect *data* about pollution in the school environment.
The *data* show that smokers die younger than non-smokers.

data handling
noun
تداول البيانات

The process of recording and displaying data with tables, charts and graphs

Data handling is an important skill that science students must learn.
The students used their *data-handling* skills to present their results as a bar chart.

data logging
noun
تسجيل البيانات

The use of sensors connected to a computer to record data automatically

The teacher shows the class how to connect the *data logging* equipment to record the temperature and light levels.
The *data logging* software plots a graph on the computer display.

day *noun*
يوم

The time for the Earth to rotate once on its axis (24 hours); also the period when the Sun is above the horizon and it is light

The Earth's rotation causes the Sun to rise and to set once each *day*.
When it is *day* on the side of the Earth facing the Sun, it is night on the opposite side.

decay *verb*
يَتَحلل

To rot away

Bacteria, fungi, worms and other decomposers make fallen leaves *decay*.
Many plastics do not *decay* naturally in the soil – they are not biodegradable.

decibel

Sound level in decibels (dB)

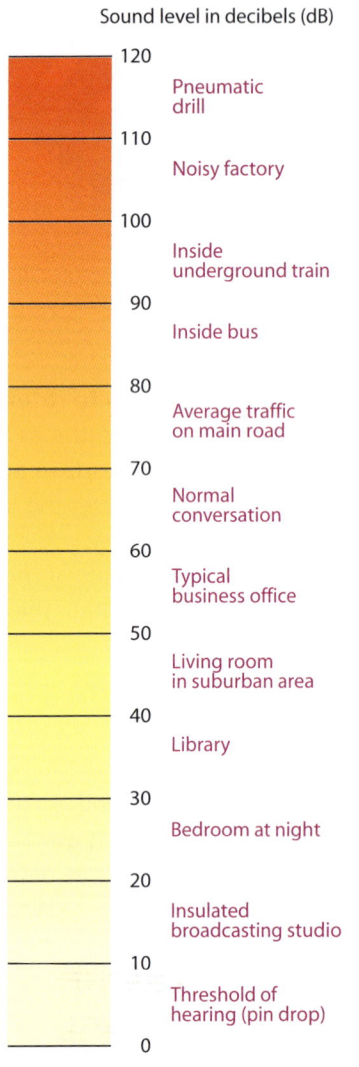

dB	
120	Pneumatic drill
110	Noisy factory
100	Inside underground train
90	Inside bus
80	Average traffic on main road
70	Normal conversation
60	Typical business office
50	Living room in suburban area
40	Library
30	Bedroom at night
20	Insulated broadcasting studio
10	Threshold of hearing (pin drop)
0	

decibel *noun* وحدة قياس شدّة الصّوت ديسبل:
A unit for measuring the loudness of sound
Prolonged exposure to sound levels greater than 90 *decibels* can damage your hearing.
The abbreviation for *decibel* is dB.

decomposer *noun* كائن محلل
A living thing that feeds on the remains of other living things, making them decay
Worms, bacteria and fungi are *decomposers*.
The *decomposers* in an ecosystem return minerals and nutrients to the soil.

deficiency disease *noun*
مرض النقص / مرض ناشئ عن سوء التغذية
A disease caused by the lack of one or more nutrients in the diet
Lack of vitamin D causes the *deficiency disease* rickets.
Many children in developing countries suffer from *deficiency diseases*.

deforestation
noun إزالة الغابات
The destruction of forests
Logging and agriculture have led to widespread *deforestation*.
Deforestation threatens wonderful animals such as the orang-utan by destroying their habitats

a
b
c
d
e
f
g
h
i
j
k
l
m
n
o
p
q
r
s
t
u
v
w
x
y
z

degree *noun* درجة

Unit into which some measurement scales are divided

The Celsius temperature scale is divided into 100 *degrees* between the freezing point and the boiling point of water.

A 90 *degree* (90°) angle is called a 'right angle'.

dehydration

noun جفاف

When the water content of a living thing is less than it should be

In hot weather, you must drink more water to avoid *dehydration*.

Severe diarrhoea and sickness can lead to life-threatening *dehydration*.

diabetes

noun السكري / مرض السكري

A disease in which the body's cells cannot absorb glucose (sugar) from blood to obtain energy

Diabetes may be caused by a lack of a substance called insulin.

Obesity is a risk factor for developing *diabetes* in later life.

diet *noun* نظام غذائي

The mixture of different foods that a person normally eats

A healthy *diet* includes several portions of fruit and vegetables each day.

A *diet* with too many cakes, cookies and sweets will make you put on weight.

desert *noun* صحراء

A region with very little rainfall

The Sahara Desert in North Africa is the largest *desert* in the world.

The world's driest place is the Atacama *Desert* in Chile; in some parts of this desert it never rains.

differentiate

differentiate *verb*   يميِّز / يفرق بين

To become different; to identify differences between things

As the embryo develops, its cells *differentiate*; some become muscle cells, others nerve cells.

You can use the litmus test to *differentiate* acids from alkalis.

---

digestion *noun*   هضم

The process in which the body breaks down food into simpler substances that it can absorb and use

During *digestion*, chemicals called enzymes break protein, carbohydrate and fat molecules into smaller pieces.

Digestion starts in the mouth as we chew our food and mix it with saliva.

digestive system

noun   الجهاز الهضمي

The mouth, oesophagus, stomach, intestines and other organs that process and digest the food we eat

The organs of the *digestive system* link together as a tube called the alimentary canal.

Food enters the *digestive system* through the mouth; waste leaves the system through the anus.

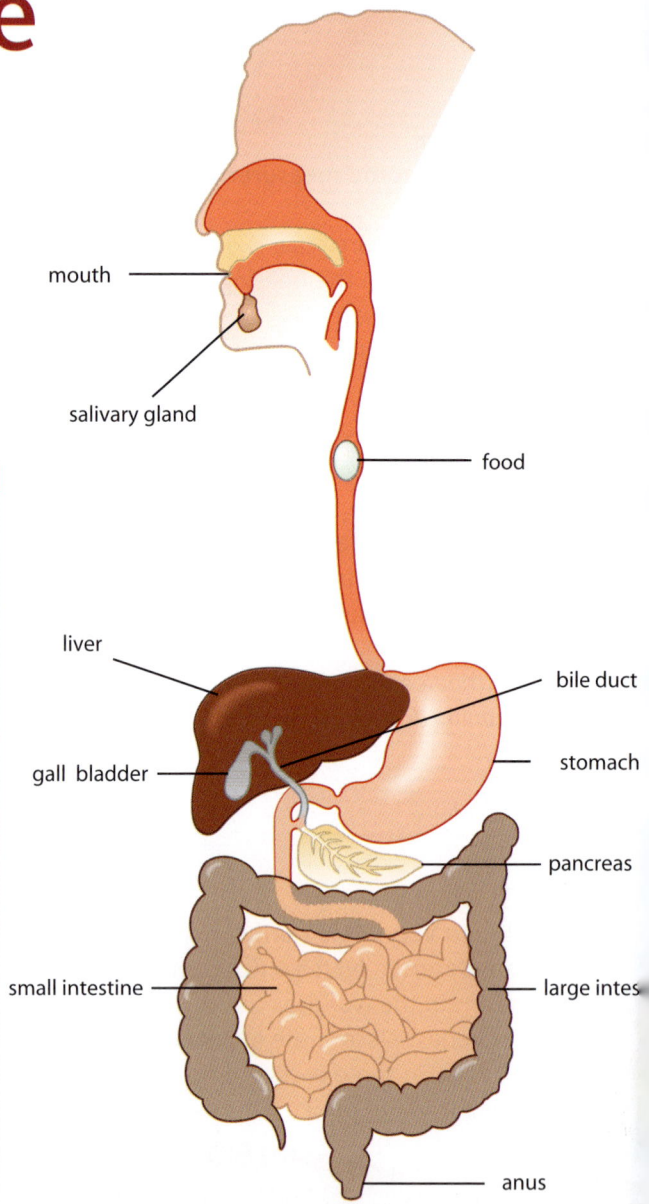

mouth

salivary gland

food

liver

bile duct

gall bladder

stomach

pancreas

small intestine

large intes

anus

disease *noun*   مرض

A disorder of the body that has not been caused by physical injury

Infectious *diseases* are caused by viruses, bacteria or other organisms that invade the body.

Lung cancer is usually a lifestyle *disease*, caused by smoking tobacco.

dispersal *noun* الانتثار

The method by which seeds are spread from a plant

Animals, wind and moving water are agents of seed *dispersal* for some plants. Mechanical *dispersal* occurs as seed pods dry and burst – scattering seeds a metre or more from the plant.

dispersion *noun* تشتّت/تقزُّح

When a mixture of different light colours is separated into a spectrum (rainbow)

Dispersion takes place as sunlight passes through raindrops.

You can see colours produced by *dispersion* when white light is reflected from the surface of a CD.

dissolve *verb* يذوب

To mix into a liquid and to become part of a solution

Salt and sugar *dissolve* in water.

When a substance *dissolves*, its molecules separate and spread.

diurnal *adjective* نهاري

Active in daylight

A *diurnal* animal feeds during the day and sleeps at night.

Owls are nocturnal, but most birds are *diurnal*.

divide *verb* يَقسِم / يَنْقسِم

To split into two or more parts

The cells *divide* every few hours.

Divide your soil sample into four equal parts.

DNA *noun* الحمض النّووي

Long spiral molecules found in the nuclei of living cells

DNA stands for deoxyribonucleic acid.

DNA molecules carry the instructions (the genes) that control cells.

domestic waste

noun قمامة/نفايات

Everyday materials that we throw away including used packaging, newspapers, broken items and food waste

Domestic waste is a common source of pollution.

We should re-use items and recycle materials to reduce the amount of *domestic waste* we produce.

drugs *plural noun* دواء

Substances that people take to cure illness, relieve pain or change their mood

Medicines are *drugs* that fight illness.

Taking illegal *drugs* can cause illness or even death.

Ee

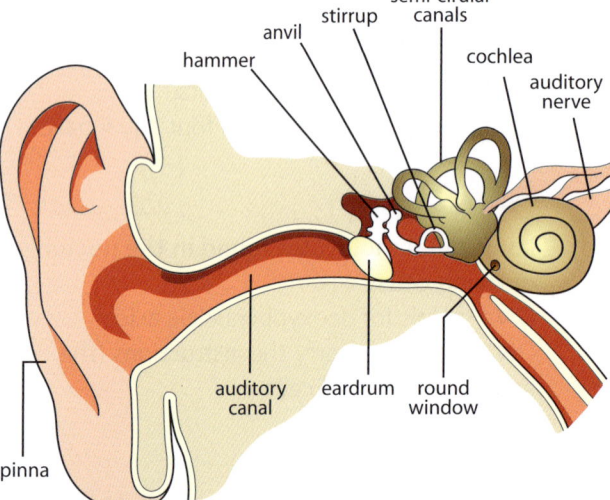

semi-cirular canals
stirrup
anvil
hammer
cochlea
auditory nerve

auditory canal
eardrum
round window

pinna

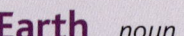

Earth *noun*   الكرة الأرضية
The planet on which we live
The *Earth* is the third planet from the Sun.
Oceans cover nearly three-quarters of the *Earth's* surface.

earthquake *noun*   زلزال
Shaking of the ground caused by sudden movements of the Earth's crust
A major *earthquake* causes widespread destruction and loss of life.
Earthquakes are most frequent along fault lines where the Earth's plates move against each other.

ear *noun*   أُذُن
The sense organ we use to hear sounds
Sounds enter the *ear* through the *ear* canal.
We have two *ears* to help us judge the direction of a sound source.

eardrum *noun*   طبلة الأذن
A piece of stretched skin that vibrates when sound enters the ear
The *eardrum* transmits sound vibrations to tiny bones called ossicles.
The sound of a nearby explosion could damage your *eardrums*.

eclipse
noun   كسوف الشمس / خسوف القمر
When the light from the Sun is blocked by the Moon or the Earth
In a solar *eclipse*, the Moon passes over the face of the Sun, blocking its light.
In a lunar *eclipse*, the Earth's shadow falls on the Moon.

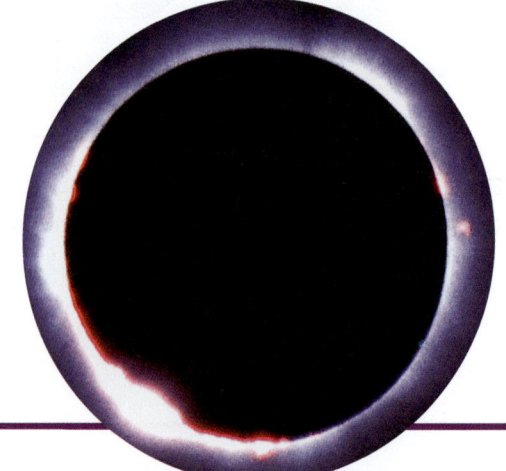

ecology *noun* علم البيئة

The science of how living things interact with each other and their surroundings

Scientists investigate the *ecology* of rain forests.

In *ecology*, a consumer is a living thing that eats plants.

ecosystem *noun* النظام البيئي

A community of living things that sustains itself in its environment

The plants, animals, fungi and microbes of the rain forest *ecosystem* depend on each other for survival.

In a pond *ecosystem*, water plants are the producers; snails, frogs and fish are consumers; microbes and worms are decomposers.

efficient *adjective* فعّال

Describes something that performs its function without waste

An energy-*efficient* light bulb wastes less energy than an old-fashioned light bulb.

A well-oiled bicycle is more *efficient* than a rusty one.

egestion *noun*
طرح الطعام غير المهضوم (قيء / تبرز)

When a living thing gets rid of undigested food from its body

Defecation and vomiting are examples of *egestion*.

Egestion should not be confused with excretion.

elastic *adjective* مرن

Describes a material that springs back to shape after being squashed or bent

Rubber is a highly *elastic* material.

A spring is *elastic* provided you do not stretch it too much – springs are used to make trampolines.

elastic energy

noun طاقة المرونة

Energy stored by a spring, a rubber band or another material when a force temporarily changes its shape

The model airplane was powered by the *elastic energy* stored in a twisted rubber band.

As the ball bounces, its kinetic energy is converted to *elastic energy*, then back to kinetic energy.

electricity

a
b
c
d
e
f
g
h
i
j
k
l
m
n
o
p
q
r
s
t
u
v
w
x
y
z

electricity *noun*   كهرباء

Anything to do with electric charge, particularly the use of electric energy
Electricity powers light bulbs, kettles, televisions, computers and many other appliances.
A lightning strike is a natural demonstration of the power of *electricity*.

electric charge *noun* شحنة كهربية

A property of some of the particles in atoms that causes them to attract or repel; there are two types of charge – positive and negative
A toy balloon can be given an *electric charge* by rubbing it with a woollen cloth.
The law of *electric charge* is that like charges repel, unlike charges attract.

repel   repel   attract

electromagnet
noun   مغناطيس كهربائي

A magnet made by passing an electric current through a coil of wire
An *electromagnet* may be switched on or off.
The strength of an *electromagnet* is increased if the wire is wrapped around an iron core.

electron *noun*   إلكترون

A tiny particle that is a component of every atom
The atoms of different elements have different numbers of *electrons*.
Every *electron* has a negative electric charge.

Copper

Tin

Zinc

Lithium

Iron

element *noun*   عنصر

A pure substance made from a single type of atom
Oxygen, silicon and aluminium are the most common *elements* in the Earth's crust.
There are 90 naturally occurring *elements*; hydrogen (*element* 1) is the lightest and uranium (*element* 92) is the heaviest.

emit *verb*   يُصدِر/ يُشع

To give out
A light source *emits* light; a sound source *emits* sound.
A dull dark surface *emits* more heat energy than a white or shiny surface.

equipment

energy

noun   طاقة

Something has energy when it can do work or cause change

Fuels such as oil and gas are the main *energy* source for transport and industry.

We obtain the *energy* our bodies need from the food we eat.

enquiry   *noun*   استقصاء/تحقيق

The process of asking questions and making investigations

Scientific *enquiry* requires careful planning.

In a scientific *enquiry,* observations are recorded and interpreted.

environment   *noun*   بيئة

All the living and non-living things that create the surroundings of a particular place

The city is a man-made *environment*.

Forests, deserts and coral reefs are natural *environments*.

epicentre / epicenter

noun   مركز الزلزال

The point on the ground immediately above the focus of an earthquake

The *epicentre* of the earthquake was 20 km from the city centre.

There was some damage to buildings within a radius of 50 km of the *epicentre*.

epidemic   *noun*   وبائي

An outbreak of many more cases of a disease than is normal

Water pollution by human waste caused a cholera *epidemic* in the city.

Vaccination prevents *epidemics* of childhood diseases such as measles and mumps.

equipment

noun   معدات / تجهيزات

Apparatus and instruments used for experiments and investigations

Make a list of the *equipment* you will need for your project.

Use simple *equipment* such as collecting jars, a ruler and a magnifying glass to investigate your environment.

erosion

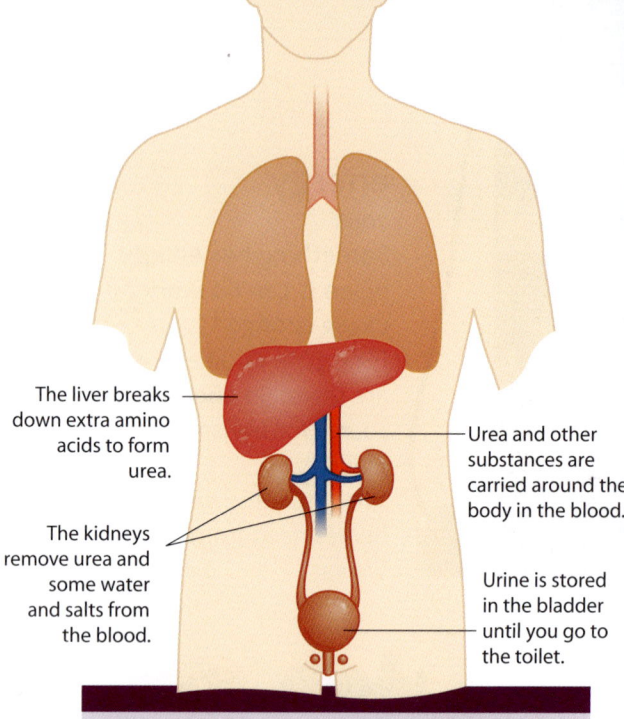

erosion *noun* تآكُل
When something (soil or rock, for example) is worn away
Erosion by running water has cut a deep gorge into the rock.
Tree roots prevent *erosion* by holding the soil in place.

evacuate *verb* يُفرغ/يُخلي
To empty – of air or of people, for example
Robert Hooke used a pump to *evacuate* the glass jar containing the watch; the watch's tick could no longer be heard.
A tsunami early warning system allows people to *evacuate* the coastline before the wave strikes.

evaporate
verb يتبخر
To change from liquid to vapour at a temperature below the boiling point
The wet washing dries as the water *evaporates* into the air.
The heat of the Sun causes water to *evaporate* from the oceans.

evidence *noun* دليل
Observations, measurements and other facts that indicate, or support, an explanation
Scientific theories are based on *evidence*.
Evidence that the Universe is expanding comes from measurements of the light from distant galaxies.

The liver breaks down extra amino acids to form urea.

Urea and other substances are carried around the body in the blood.

The kidneys remove urea and some water and salts from the blood.

Urine is stored in the bladder until you go to the toilet.

excretion *noun* إخراج
When a living thing gets rid of waste substances formed by the chemical reactions in its cells
Excretion takes place as we urinate, sweat and exhale (breathe out).
Scientists do not classify defecation as *excretion* because the waste material in our faeces did not take part in the body's life processes.

excretory system
noun جهاز الإخراج
The kidneys, bladder, lungs, skin and other organs that filter and pass waste from the body
The kidneys are the *excretory system's* filters; they remove waste materials from the blood.
The lungs form part of the *excretory system* by removing waste gases from the body as we exhale (breathe out).

eye

a
b
c
d
e
f
g
h
i
j
k
l
m
n
o
p
q
r
s
t
u
v
w
x
y
z

experiment *noun* تجربة
A practical test or investigation carried out by a scientist
In this *experiment*, you will compare the strengths of different materials.
Devise an *experiment* to test the theory that plants grow towards light.

exercise *noun* تدريب/تمرين
Activity that keeps the body fit and healthy
Swimming, walking, cycling and team games are good forms of *exercise*.
Regular *exercise* helps control your weight and keep your heart strong.

expand *verb* يتمدّد
To increase in length or volume; to get bigger
A gas *expands* to fill its container.
As the temperature rises, the liquid in the thermometer bulb *expands*.

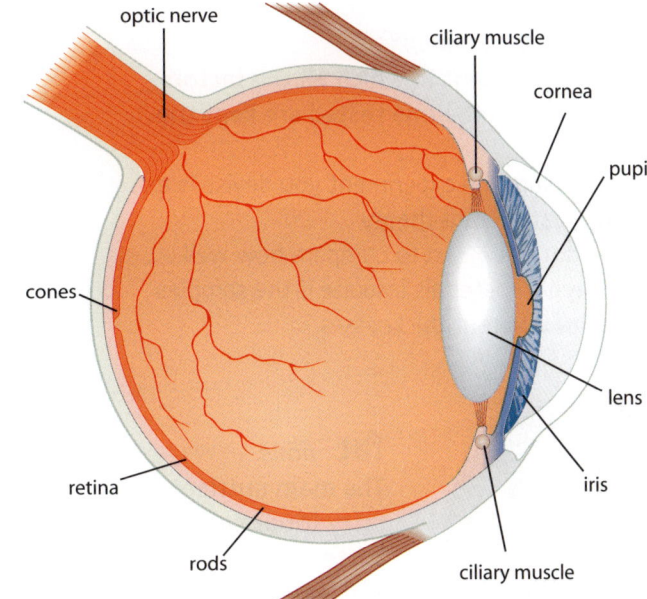

optic nerve

ciliary muscle

cornea

pupil

cones

lens

retina

iris

rods

ciliary muscle

eye *noun* عين
The sense organ we use to see
The *eye* works in a similar way to a camera.
We see when light bounces from the objects around us into our *eyes.*

Ff

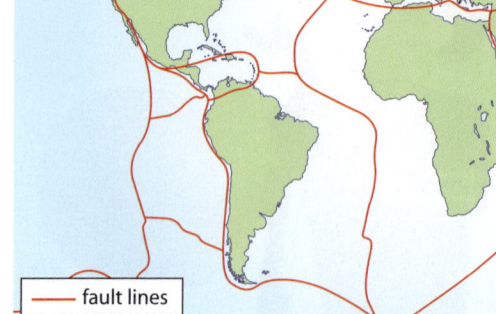

— fault lines

factor *noun*

عامل/مُتغيِّر

One of the things that influence the outcome of an experiment or process; may also be called a 'variable'

Temperature and rainfall are two *factors* that affect plant growth.

Which *factor* is more affected by diet – waist size or shoe size?

fair test *noun*

اختبار عادل

An experiment in which all the factors apart from the one tested are kept the same

Make sure the experiment you devise is a *fair test* of your theory.

It's not a *fair test* to compare how well different materials insulate if the samples are of different thicknesses.

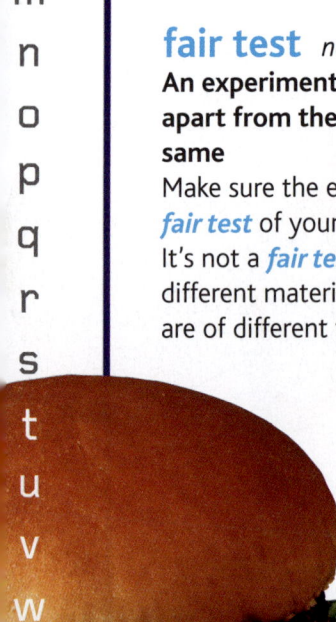

fat *noun*

دهن

The main nutrient in fatty foods such as butter, cooking oil and lard

High-*fat* foods have a high calorie content.

Too much *fat* in the diet can cause weight gain and heart problems.

fault *noun*

صدع

A line along which parts of the Earth's crust have slipped relative to each other

The San Andreas *Fault* runs close to the city of San Francisco.

Earthquakes and volcanic activity are common along *fault* lines.

fermentation *noun*

تخمُّر

The action of yeast and bacteria when feeding on sugars in food products

Fermentation by yeast produces the gas carbon dioxide which makes bread dough rise.

Cheese and yoghurt are produced by the *fermentation* of milk.

fertile *adjective*

خِصب

Describes soil that contains everything needed for plants to grow well; also describes a living thing which is able to reproduce

A *fertile* soil is rich in humus.

The farmer ploughs manure and compost into the soil to make it more *fertile*.

The *fertile* plants produced flowers which became fruit.

fertilisation / fertilization

noun   إخصاب

The moment when a male reproductive cell combines with a female reproductive cell

Once the flower has been pollinated, *fertilisation* takes place.

Following *fertilisation*, the embryo begins to develop.

fibre

noun   ليف (مُفرَد أليَاف)

Material in the form of a thin strand

Fabrics are woven from both natural and man-made *fibres*.

A mass of soft *fibres* protects cotton seeds in the seed pods.

filament (biology)   *noun*   خيط (أحياء)

The thin stalk that supports the anther in the male part of a flower

The anther and the *filament* together make the stamen.

filament (electricity)

noun   فتيلة (كهرباء)

The fine wire in a light bulb that glows white hot as an electric current passes through it

Modern light bulb *filaments* are made from the metal tungsten.

filter   *noun*   مرشِّح

Something used to separate a mixture that is passed through it

The students made a *filter* with filter paper and a funnel.

An air *filter* traps dust particles as air is blown through.

A red colour *filter* only allows red light to pass through; other colours are absorbed.

filtrate   *noun*   رشيح

Liquid that has been passed through a filter to remove solid particles

The students collected the *filtrate* in a beaker placed under the funnel.

The *filtrate* appears much less cloudy than the original mixture.

filtration

noun   ترشيح

The process of separating solid particles from a liquid by using a filter

A mixture of sand and water can be separated by *filtration*.

At a water treatment plant, *filtration* through sand removes small solid particles from the water.

first aid   *noun*   إسعافات أولية

Emergency medical treatment

The first rule of *first aid* is to keep calm.

At the *first-aid* course the students learnt how to treat minor injuries.

a b c d e **f** g h i j k l m n o p q r s t u v w x y z

fish

fish *noun*　　سمك

A vertebrate animal with cold blood that lives and reproduces in water

Fish swim with the aid of fins.

Fish are able to absorb oxygen dissolved in water through their gills.

flexible *adjective* مرن

Describes a material that is easy to bend

A belt must be made from a *flexible* material such as leather.

The plastic ruler was more *flexible* than the wooden ruler.

float *verb* يطفو

To rest on the surface of water

Objects *float* if they are lighter for their size than water.

When an object *floats*, its weight is exactly balanced by the upthrust from the water it pushes aside.

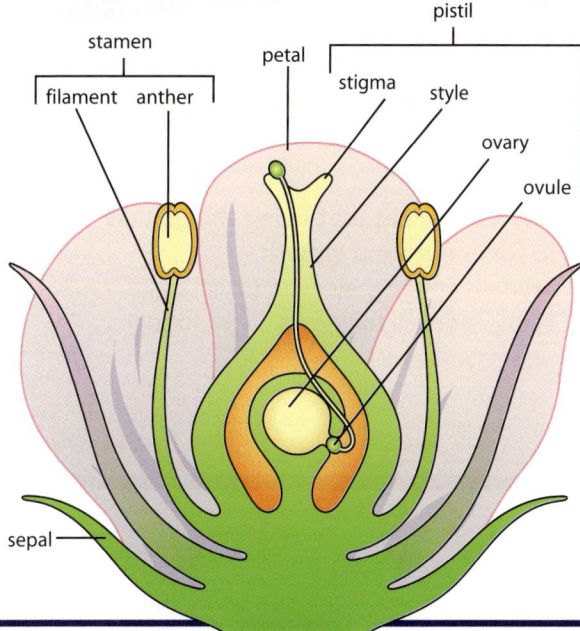

focus (earthquake) *noun* بؤرة (الزلزال)

The centre or origin of an earthquake

The *focus* of an earthquake is underground, directly below the epicentre.

Powerful vibrations spread in all directions from the *focus* and can damage buildings.

flood *verb* يفيض

When water covers a place that is usually dry

Heavy rains in the mountains cause rivers to *flood* the fields along their banks.

As the ice caps melt the rising sea will *flood* coastal towns and villages.

flower *noun* زهرة

The part of a plant that makes seeds

The *flower* is the plant's reproductive organ.

Brightly coloured *flowers* attract birds and insects.

stamen
filament anther
petal
pistil
stigma style
ovary
ovule
sepal

fetus / foetus

fetus/foetus *noun* جنين
A baby developing in the womb
Eight weeks after fertilisation the embryo develops features and becomes a *fetus*. At 12 weeks, the *fetus* is about as long as your little finger.

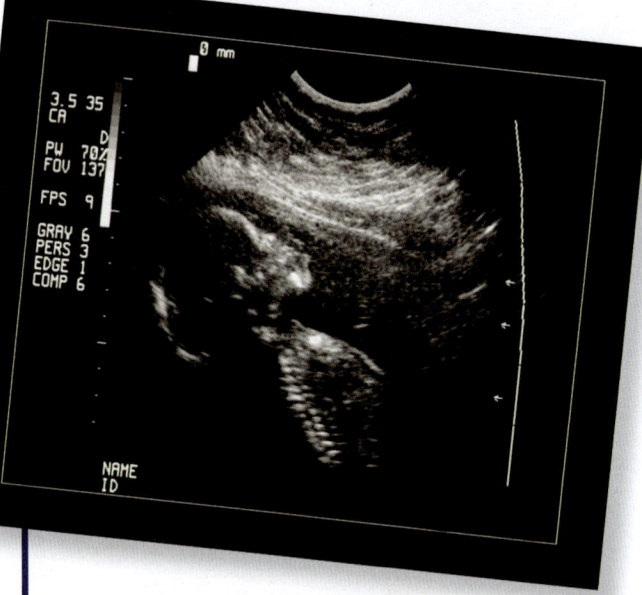

food *noun* غذاء
The substances that living things take in for energy and growth
Animals obtain their *food* by eating. Plants produce their own *food* through photosynthesis.

Sun

food chain
noun السلسلة الغذائية
A chart that shows how the energy of food passes from one living thing to another as they feed
Almost every *food chain* starts with a green plant. In a *food chain*, plants are the producers and animals the consumers.

plant

food web
noun شبكة غذائية
A diagram that shows how the food chains in an ecosystem link together
In the desert *food web*, the cheetah and eagle are top predators. Most of the energy that supports the pond *food web* is provided by algae floating at the water surface.

herbivore

carnivore

force *noun* قوة
A push or pull that tends to change the motion of an object
The *force* of gravity pulls all objects towards the ground.
The *force* of friction always opposes motion.

fungi

fossil *noun*   أحفورة/مُستحاثة

The buried remains of a living thing preserved as stone

We learn about dinosaurs by studying their *fossils*.

Scientists can judge the age of sedimentary rocks from the *fossils* they contain.

fossil fuel *noun*   وقود أحفوري

A fuel created from the buried remains of plants and animals by the action of pressure and heat

Coal, oil and natural gas are *fossil fuels*.
Burning *fossil fuels* releases greenhouse gases into the atmosphere.

freeze *verb*   يتجمد

To change state from liquid to solid

Water *freezes* to ice at 0°C.
In cold climates, rivers and lakes *freeze* in the winter.

friction *noun*   احتكاك

The force that opposes motion when one surface slides or tends to slide over another

You can feel *friction* warming your hands as you rub them together.

Friction between your shoes and the floor prevents you from slipping.

fuel *noun*   وقود

A substance that is burnt to provide heat or power

In developing countries, wood and charcoal are the main *fuels* used for cooking.

At the oil refinery, petrol, diesel, kerosene and other *fuels* are separated from crude oil by fractional distillation.

fungi *plural noun*   فطريّات

The kingdom of living things that includes mushrooms and toadstools

Fungi obtain nutrition by absorbing the rotting remains of other living things.

Moulds and yeasts are microscopic *fungi*.

Gg

a
b
c
d
e
f
g
h
i
j
k
l
m
n
o
p
q
r
s
t
u
v
w
x
y
z

generator *noun*   مُولّد كهرباء
A machine that transforms motion energy into electrical energy
At a hydroelectric power plant, moving water powers the *generators*.
A portable *generator* provides electricity in an emergency.

galaxy *noun*   مجرة
A cluster of billions of stars in space
Our solar system is in the *galaxy* we call the Milky Way.
The next nearest galaxy to the Milky Way is called the Andromeda *Galaxy*; it is the most distant object you can see with the naked eye.

gas *noun*   غاز
The thinnest, lightest state of matter
Steam is water in the *gas* state.
The particles in a *gas* are widely separated and move freely.

gene *noun*   جين/وحدة وراثيّة
A unit of information stored by the DNA in living cells
Genes are the instructions that guide how a living thing grows.
The characteristics of parents are transmitted to offspring by the *genes* in reproductive cells.

germination *noun*   إنبات
When a new plant starts to grow from a seed
Germination does not require light; it takes place under the soil.
Water and warmth are required for *germination*.

global warming *noun*   الاحترار العالمي
The increase in the average temperature of the Earth, caused by greenhouse gases trapping heat in the Earth's atmosphere
Increased use of fossil fuels may be linked to *global warming*.
If *global warming* continues, the Earth's climate will change.

growth

(graph y-axis) melting point °C

200
180
160
140
120
100
80
60
40
20
0

Li   Na   K

alkali metal

Some of the radiation emitted by the Earth escapes into space.

Some of the radiation is absorbed by gases in the atmosphere. These warm gases help to keep the Earth warm.

The Sun is very hot. Infared radiation from the Sun can pass through the atmosphere.

The Earth is not as hot as the Sun. The infared radiation it emits does not have as much energy.

graph *noun*   رسم بياني
A chart that shows how one factor depends on another
The *graph* shows how the plant's height increased with time.
Plot a *graph* to show how the sea temperature changes during the year.

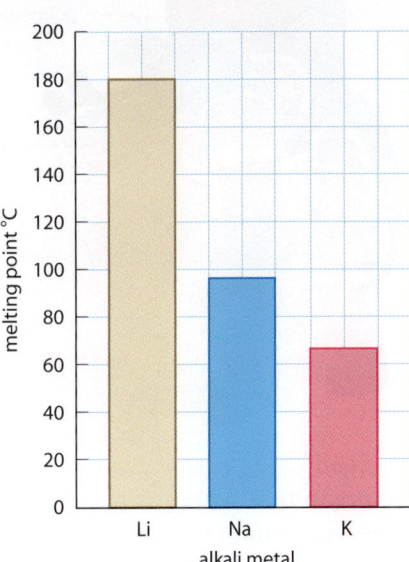

grassland
noun   أرض عشبية
A biome in which grass and other low plants are the main vegetation
Lions, giraffes, zebra and wildebeest are *grassland* animal species.
In Africa, *grassland* is called 'savannah'.

gravity *noun*   جاذبية
The force that pulls objects with mass together
On Earth, the force of *gravity* pulls objects towards the ground; it gives them weight.
The planets are held in their orbits around the Sun by the force of *gravity*.

greenhouse effect
noun   ظاهرة الدفيئة/الاحتباس الحراري
The effect of certain gases in the Earth's atmosphere, which trap heat as glass does in a greenhouse
Without the *greenhouse effect* the Earth would be much cooler.
An increase in the *greenhouse effect* is raising the Earth's average temperature.

greenhouse gas
noun   غازات الدفيئة/الاحتباس الحراري
A gas that contributes to the greenhouse effect
Methane is a *greenhouse gas*.
When fuels burn they release the *greenhouse gas* carbon dioxide into the atmosphere.

growth *noun*   نمو
An increase in size
Growth is most rapid during infancy.
Teenagers experience a *growth* spurt during puberty.

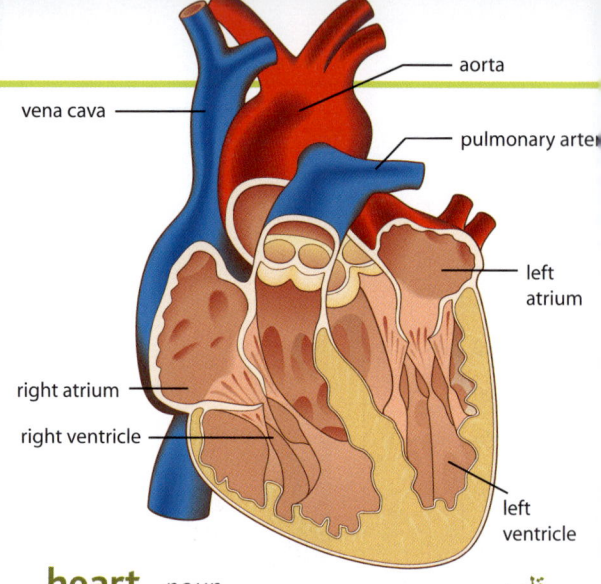

aorta

vena cava

pulmonary arter[y]

left atrium

right atrium

right ventricle

left ventricle

Hh

habitat *noun*   موطن

The surroundings or environment in which an organism normally lives

The worm's *habitat* is the soil.
Many species are threatened by the destruction of their *habitat*.

hardness *noun*   صلابة

The measure of how well a material resists scratching

Hardness is one of the factors that help a geologist identify a rock sample.
On Moh's *hardness* scale, diamond is the hardest mineral; talc is the softest.

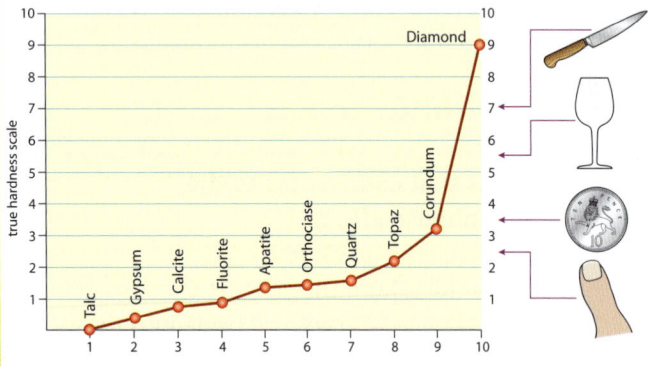

health *noun*   صحة

The condition of the body and mind; whether you are well or ill

A balanced diet and regular exercise are important for good *health*.
Choosing not to smoke is one of the best decisions you can make for your *health*.

heart *noun*   قلب

The body organ that works as a pump to circulate blood around the body

The human *heart* beats about once a second.
When you exercise your *heart* rate increases.

heat *verb*   حرارة

To transfer heat energy to something

Heat the sample gently over a Bunsen burner.
Reptiles *heat* their bodies by basking in the Sun.

heat energy *noun*   طاقة حرارية

The form of energy that makes things hot (gives them a high temperature)

In a power station, *heat energy* from burning fuel is used to boil water.
As the car brakes, friction transforms its motion energy into *heat energy*.

heat source *noun*   مصدر حراري

Something that releases heat energy

Clothes irons, hair dryers and cookers are *heat sources* that we use in the home.
The Sun is the *heat source* for life on Earth.

herbivore   *noun*   آكل الأعشاب

An animal that eats only plants

Grazing animals such as sheep and cattle are *herbivores*.

In a food chain a *herbivore* is the primary consumer.

hereditary   *adjective*   وراثي

Describes a characteristic or condition (a disease, for example) which may pass from parents to offspring

Eye colour is *hereditary*.

The language we speak is not *hereditary*; we learn it as we grow up.

hereditary disease

noun   مرض وراثي

A disease that may pass in the genes from a parent to a child

The *hereditary disease* called sickle cell anaemia affects the shape of red blood cells.

Haemophilia is a *hereditary disease* that may pass from a mother to her son.

heterogeneous / heterogenous

adjective   غير متجانس

Describes a mixture in which you can see different components

Soil is a *heterogeneous* mixture of different-sized particles.

A mixture of salt and sand is *heterogeneous*, but a solution of salt in water is homogeneous.

HIV

noun

فيروس مرض نقص المناعة

Human immunodeficiency virus

HIV is the virus that causes the condition called AIDS.

HIV is transmitted in infected blood.

homogeneous / homogenous

adjective   متجانس

Describes a mixture which appears the same throughout

A solution is a *homogeneous* mixture.

Stir the ingredients until the mixture appears *homogeneous*.

host   *noun*   عائل

The organism on which a parasite lives

Head lice are parasites; they feed on the blood of their human *host*.

A parasite may harm its *host*, but usually it does not kill it.

humidity

humidity *noun* رطوبة
The measure of the amount of water vapour in the air
The *humidity* is high in the rain forest and low in the desert.
High *humidity* is very uncomfortable; sweat cannot evaporate to cool your body.

humus *noun* دبال
The rotted remains of living things in soil
Humus is formed by the action of worms and other decomposers.
Fertile soils contain plenty of *humus*.

hygiene *noun* النظافة
Cleanliness; keeping clean and germ-free
Good *hygiene* is an important part of a healthy lifestyle.
Poor *hygiene* in the kitchen spreads germs into food.

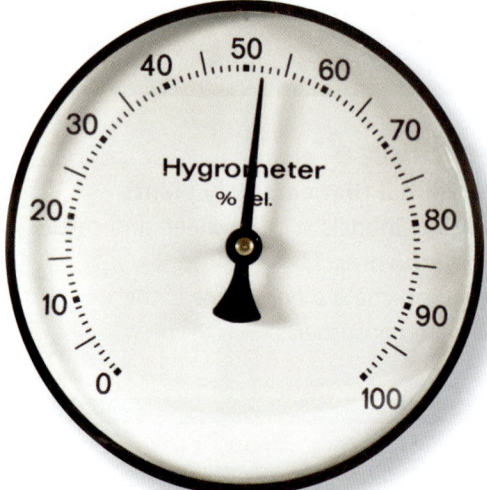

hygrometer *noun* المرطاب / جهاز قياس الرطوبة
A weather instrument that records humidity
The student recorded the reading on the *hygrometer*.
The humidity reading on the *hygrometer* was 50 per cent.

hurricane *noun* إعصار
A tropical storm with winds speeds above 119 km/h
The *hurricane* caused widespread damage to buildings.
In some parts of the world, *hurricane*-force winds are called 'typhoons'.

hypothesis *noun* افتراض / فرض
An explanation or theory that has yet to be proved
One *hypothesis* is that the extinction of the dinosaurs was caused by a volcano.
Edward Jenner made the *hypothesis* that infection with cowpox gave immunity to smallpox.

Ii

ice *noun* ثلج
Water in the solid state
Liquid water freezes to solid *ice* at 0°C.
A glacier is a river of *ice*.

ICT *noun* تقنيات المعلومات والاتصالات
Information and communication technologies
ICT is the use of computers to handle data.
Use your *ICT* skills to display and print your data in the form of a pie chart.

igneous *adjective* ناري/بركاني
Describes rocks that have been formed by the cooling of molten rocks
Igneous rocks are usually hard, dark and composed of small, shiny crystals.
Lava from a volcano cools to form *igneous* rock.

image *noun* صورة
A picture of the surroundings formed with light
The camera lens focuses an *image* onto the light sensor.
The *image* in a plane mirror is back to front compared with the object.

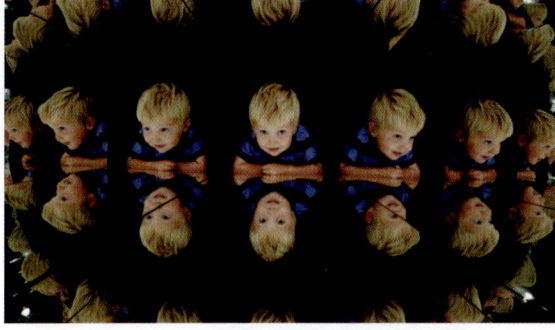

incidence *noun* سقوط
When light or something else strikes a surface
The angle of *incidence* is equal to the angle of reflection.
Measure the angle of refraction for different angles of *incidence*.

inclined plane

inclined plane *noun*   مسطح مائل

A ramp or a sloping surface used as a simple machine

It is easier to push a load gradually up an *inclined plane* than to lift it vertically.
A wedge is a small *inclined plane* that you can use to jam a door open or split a log.

indicator *noun*   مؤشر / دليل

A substance that changes colour to show if a solution is acid or alkaline

Note the colour change when you dip the *indicator* paper in the solution.
Litmus is an *indicator* that turns red in an acid and blue in an alkali.

infancy *noun*   مرحلة المهد

The first stage of early childhood

Growth is most rapid during *infancy*.
During *infancy*, a baby learns to sit up and crawl, and may say its first word.

infectious *adjective*   مُعدي

Describes a disease that passes from one living thing to another; an infectious disease is one that we can 'catch'

Influenza is most *infectious* during the first few days in which you have symptoms.
Avoid contact with others during the *infectious* period.

insect

insect *noun*

حشرة

An invertebrate animal whose adult stage has six legs

Beetles are by far the most numerous *insect* group.

An adult *insect* has three main body parts; many insects have wings and can fly.

insoluble

insoluble *adjective* غير قابل للذوبان

Describes a substance that does not dissolve

Sand is *insoluble* in water.

Salt is soluble in water but *insoluble* in oil.

insulate *verb* يعزل

To prevent heat (or electricity) from entering or leaving something, or to use an insulator to prevent heat loss or gain

We should *insulate* our homes to keep them cool in summer and warm in winter.

Electric wires are *insulated* with plastic to prevent short circuits and shocks.

insulator *noun* عازل

A material that does not carry heat and/or electricity well

Metals are good conductors, but most plastics are *insulators*.

A saucepan handle made from a heat *insulator* such as wood or plastic does not get too hot to hold.

invertebrate *noun* لا فقاري

An animal without a backbone

Worms and molluscs are soft-bodied *invertebrates*.

Arthropods are *invertebrates* with a hard skin, jointed legs and a body divided into segments.

investigate *verb* يستقصي/يبحث

To study something in detail; to try to find the facts

In this project, you will *investigate* the effects of heat on materials.

Discuss how you could *investigate* pollution around your school.

iris *noun* الحدقة/القزحيّة

The coloured ring that surrounds the pupil in the eye

The *iris* controls the size of the pupil.

The human *iris* may be brown, blue, green or hazel in colour.

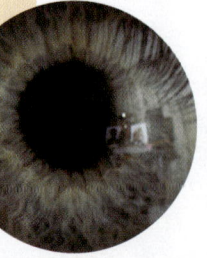
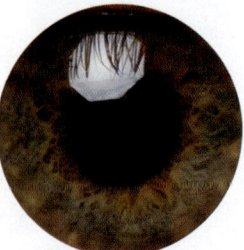
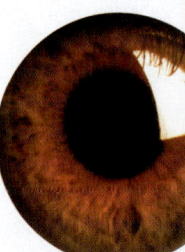

Kk

key *noun* مفتاح/دليل

A chart or table that aids identification of items (species, for example) with a series of yes/no questions; also a table that gives the meaning of the symbol on a map or chart

Answer the questions in the *key* to help identify the invertebrates you have collected.

Make a simple *key* to identify a vertebrate as a mammal, bird, reptile, amphibian or fish.

kilogram
noun كيلوجرام

A unit of mass

The mass of 1 litre of water is 1 *kilogram*. The *kilogram* is the standard unit of mass in the International System of Units (the SI system) used by scientists.

kinetic energy
noun الطاقة الحركية

The energy of motion

A large mass has more *kinetic energy* than a smaller mass travelling at the same speed. As the stone falls, its gravitational energy is transformed into *kinetic energy*.

A speeding train has a huge quantity of *kinetic energy*.

Ll

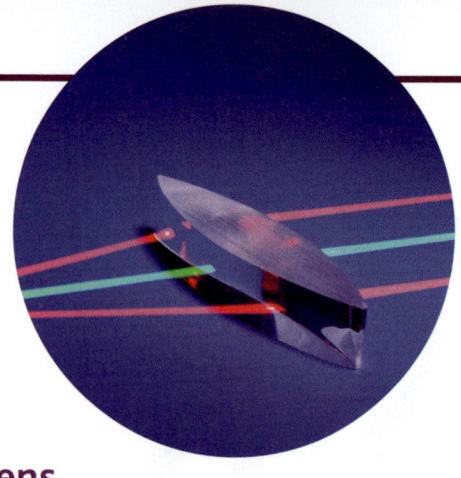

leaf
noun   ورقة نبات

A flat part of a plant that spreads to catch sunlight
The *leaf* is the main site for photosynthesis.
Gases enter and leave the *leaf* through tiny pores called stomata on its lower surface.

lens
noun   عدسة

A curved piece of transparent material shaped to concentrate or spread out light
A magnifying glass is a convex *lens*.
The *lens* in the eye focuses an image onto the retina.

lever
noun   رافعة

A rod or a bar used as a simple machine to produce movement and transmit force
With a *lever*, you can move a large load with a smaller effort. The fulcrum is the point around which the *lever* turns.

length *noun*   طول
The distance along something; the time something lasts
Use a ruler to measure the *length* of the specimen in centimetres.
Twenty-four hours is the *length* of one day.

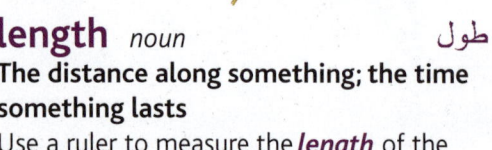

life processes
plural noun   العمليات الحيويّة

The seven things that, together, are characteristic of all living things: growth, movement, nutrition (feeding), respiration (breathing), reproduction, excretion and sensing
Describe how a plant shows each of the seven *life processes*.
A non-living thing may show some *life processes*, but not all seven: a river moves, for example, but it does not breathe.

locomotion

lifestyle disease

noun — مرض مرتبط بنمط المعيشة

A disease caused by the way you live your life

Eating too much fat, salt and sugar may lead to *lifestyle diseases* such as heart disease and diabetes.

You can reduce your risk of developing a *lifestyle disease* by choosing not to smoke, eating a balanced diet and taking regular exercise.

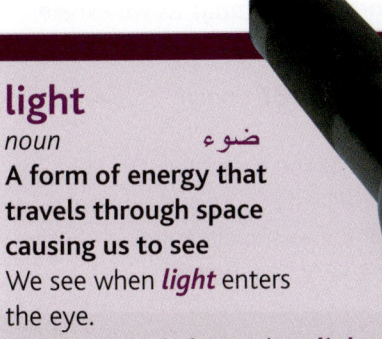

light

noun — ضوء

A form of energy that travels through space causing us to see

We see when *light* enters the eye.

Nothing travels faster than *light*; *light* is the fastest thing in the Universe.

light source   *noun* — مصدر ضوء

Something that emits (gives out) light

The Sun is the natural *light source* that gives us daylight.

At night, we use artificial *light sources* such as candles and electric lamps to give us light.

liquid   *noun* — سائل

The state of matter in which particles are closely spaced but free to move over each other

Water is the most common *liquid* on Earth.

A *liquid* flows to take the shape of its container.

living thing

noun — كائن حيّ

Something which shows all seven processes of life: movement, growth, nutrition, respiration, reproduction, excretion, sensing

A biologist is a scientist who studies *living things*.

The five kingdoms of *living things* are plants, animals, fungi, monera (bacteria) and protists.

loam   *noun* — تربة طفلية

A type of soil

Loam is a mixture of clay, sand and humus. Clay and sandy soils are less fertile than *loam*.

locomotion

noun — حركة

Movement: the way in which an animal moves

Walking, running, swimming and flying are different forms of animal *locomotion*.

Animal *locomotion* is powered by muscles.

a b c d e f g h i j k **l** m n o p q r s t u v w x y z

53

loudness

loudness *noun* شِدَّة/ارتفاع (الصّوت)
The level (strength, or volume) of sound
You can increase the *loudness* of the sound by increasing the strength of the vibrations that produce it.
Loudness is measured in decibels.

lubricant *noun* شحم
A substance that reduces friction
Without oil to act as *lubricant*, a car engine would soon seize up.
The *lubricant* forms a thin, slippery film between the moving parts of the machine.

lunar eclipse
noun خسوف القمر
When the Earth's shadow falls on the Moon
A *lunar eclipse* can only take place when the Moon is full.
During a *lunar eclipse*, the Earth lies directly between the Sun and the Moon.

lunar month
noun شهر قمري
The time between one New Moon and the next
A *lunar month* is 29 days, 12 hours and 44 minutes long.
The *lunar month* is more than 2 days longer than the time the Moon takes to complete one orbit of the Earth; this is because, in that time, the Earth has moved on in its orbit around the Sun.

lung *noun* الرئة
Body organ, consisting of two lungs, through which oxygen from the air enters the blood
As we inhale, our *lungs* expand to fill with air. Waste carbon dioxide from respiration is excreted through the *lungs* as we exhale.

lustre / luster *noun* بريق / لمعان
Shininess
Lustre is one of the characteristics that can help you to identify rocks and minerals. Chalk has a dull lustre; diamonds and other gems have a very high *lustre*.

Mm

magma *noun* الصُّهارة
Molten rock under the Earth's crust
A volcano is a place where *magma* breaks through the Earth's crust.
When *magma* cools it freezes to form igneous rock.

magnet *noun* مغناطيس
A piece of material that attracts iron and other magnetic materials through its magnetic force
Every *magnet* has two poles: a north pole and a south pole.
Suspend a bar magnet from a thread to make a *magnetic* (adjective) compass.

magnetise / magnetize *verb* يمغنط
To make into a magnet
You can *magnetise* an iron nail by stroking it with one pole of a magnet.
The electric current *magnetises* the iron bar placed inside the coil.

magnetism *noun* مغناطيسية
A force created by certain materials and by electric currents
Magnetism only acts strongly on iron and a few other metals.
The laws of *magnetism* are: like poles repel; unlike poles attract.

magnifying glass *noun* عدسة مكبّرة
A lens used to make small objects appear larger
View the specimens with a *magnifying glass*.
The lens used to make a *magnifying glass* is convex.

magnitude *noun* مقدار
The relative size or importance of something
The *magnitude* of a star is a measure of its brightness compared with other stars.
The Richter scale measures the *magnitude* of earthquakes.

malnutrition

malnutrition *noun* سوء التغذية

The condition of not having enough food to supply the body with energy and other needs

Many children in developing countries suffer from *malnutrition*.

Children suffering from *malnutrition* are underweight and lack energy.

mammal *noun* حيوان من الثدييات

A warm-blooded vertebrate animal that feeds its young with milk

Camels, rabbits, horses, whales and dolphins are *mammals*.

Many *mammals* have fur or hair on their skin.

mantle *noun* الوشاح (من طبقات الأرض)

The layer of the Earth between the crust and the core

The *mantle* is composed of hot rocks. The temperature of the *mantle* increases from 500°C just beneath the crust to more than 4000°C where it meets the core.

marine

adjective بحري

Describes anything to do with the seas or oceans

Whales and sharks are *marine* animals. *Marine* biology is the study of life in the oceans.

medium

mass *noun* كتلة

The measure of the amount of matter that makes up an object

The kilogram is the scientific unit of *mass*. All objects with *mass* are attracted by the force of gravity.

material *noun* مادة

A substance, particularly a substance used to make something

Steel and concrete are the most widely used building *materials*. Wood is a natural *material*; plastic is a synthetic material.

matter *noun* مادّة

Everything that has mass and takes up space

Solids, liquids and gases are different forms of *matter*.

Stars and planets are made from *matter*, but light and other forms of radiation are not.

measurement *noun* قياس

The process of recording an observation as a number by using an instrument with a scale; a quantity found by measurement

Use a ruler to make the length *measurement*, and a stopwatch to measure the time.

All *measurements* should be repeated to check their accuracy.

Mediterranean *adjective*
متوسطي/متعلق بالبحر الأبيض المتوسط أو بشعوبه

Describes something linked to the Mediterranean Sea and the region around it

A *Mediterranean* climate has hot dry summers and mild winters with some rain. The *Mediterranean* diet is based on foods such as tomatoes, olives and fish.

medium *noun* وسط

The substance through which something travels

Sound requires a *medium* such as air to travel, but light can travel through a vacuum. Light may be refracted when it passes from one *medium* to another – from air to glass, for example.

melt

melt *verb* ينصهر

To change state from solid to liquid
The Sun's heat *melts* the ice.
Melt the chocolate in a saucepan.

metal *noun* فلز

A dense, shiny material that conducts heat and electricity well
Iron, copper and aluminium are common *metals*; gold, silver and platinum are precious *metals*.
Mercury is the only *metal* that is liquid at room temperature.

metamorphic *adjective* متحوّل

Describes rocks that have been changed by heat and pressure
Marble is a *metamorphic* rock formed from limestone.
Metamorphic rocks are usually hard, and may contain large, shiny crystals and show bands of colour.

meteor *noun* شهاب / نيزك

A particle of rock or metal burning up as it plunges through the atmosphere
The common name for a *meteor* is a 'shooting star'.
A shower of *meteors* (about 60 an hour) called the Perseids can be seen in the night sky on 12–13 August each year.

meteorite *noun* نيزك

A meteor that reaches the ground before it is completely burnt up
About 500 *meteorites* bigger than marbles reach the ground each year.
A large *meteorite* forms a crater on impact.

meteoroid *noun* الجسيم النيزكى

A piece of rock or metal travelling through space
Meteoroids range in size from grains of sand to large boulders.
Many *meteoroids* are debris from comet tails.

metre / meter *noun*   متر

The scientific unit of length
One *metre* is divided into 100 centimetres.
The definition of the *metre* was originally
one ten-millionth of the distance from the
Equator to the North Pole.

micro-organisms

plural noun   كائن دقيق

**Living things that are so small they can
only be seen with the aid of a microscope**
Bacteria are *micro-organisms*.
Some *micro-organisms* cause disease, others
are help us digest our food.

microscope

noun   ميكروسكوب/مِجهَر

**An instrument that
produces a greatly
magnified image of an
object**
Light *microscopes* magnify
up to 1500 times; an
electron *microscope*
magnifies up to
2 000 000 times.
Antonie van Leeuwenhoek
discovered bacteria
and red blood cells
with *microscopes*
that he made himself.

mineral (geology)

noun   معدن (جيولوجيا)

A pure, non-living substance
Diamond, gypsum, calcite and quartz are
natural *minerals*.
The metal aluminium is extracted from
the *mineral* alumina.

mineral (nutrition)

noun   معدن (تغذية)

**A simple, non-organic substance that
the body needs as a nutrient**
Anaemia may be caused by a shortage of
the *mineral* iron in the diet.
Iron, calcium, potassium, sodium,
phosphorus, magnesium, zinc and iodine
are some of the important *minerals* we
need from our food.

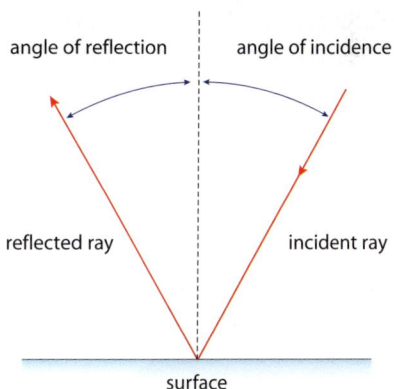

angle of reflection = angle of incidence

angle of reflection   angle of incidence

reflected ray   incident ray

surface

mirror   *noun*   مِرْآة

**A polished surface that reflects light to
produce an image**
Your image is the same distance behind the
mirror as you are in front.
The angle of reflection from a *mirror* is equal
to the angle of incidence.

a b c d e f g h i j k l **m** n o p q r s t u v w x y z

mixture

mixture *noun* مخلوط

Two or more substances that are jumbled together but have not reacted (changed)

Air is a *mixture* of nitrogen, oxygen and other gases.

Soil is a *mixture* of living and non-living things.

molecule *noun* جزيء

A group of two or more atoms held together by chemical bonds

Oxygen atoms bond in pairs to form oxygen *molecules*.

A water *molecule* consists of two atoms of hydrogen and one of oxygen.

mollusc
noun حيوان رخوي

An invertebrate animal with a soft body not divided into segments

Snails, slugs, conches, oysters, clams, mussels, octopus and squid are *molluscs*.

Molluscs have a mantle which may produce a shell; and they have a muscular foot on the underside of their body.

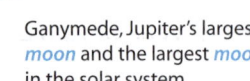

Ganymede, Jupiter's largest *moon* and the largest *moon* in the solar system

moon *noun* قمر

A large object that orbits a planet

The Earth's *moon* is a cold ball of rock.

With the aid of one of the first telescopes, Galileo discovered that Jupiter has *moons*.

motor *noun* محرك

A machine that uses an energy source to produce motion

The electric *motor* in a washing machine transforms electrical energy into motion.

The electric *motor* was invented by Michael Faraday.

musical instrument

mould (forces and materials)
verb   يُشكّل (القوى والمواد)

To make a shape in a mould or by using forces

Use your fingers and thumb to *mould* the clay.

Mould the sand to make a castle.

mould (forces and materials)
noun   قالب (القوى والمواد)

A container for casting a shape

Pour molten chocolate in the *mould* and let it cool.

The sculptor makes a *mould* with plaster.

mould (biology)   *noun*   عفن (أحياء)

A type of fungus

Patches of blue, green and grey *mould* grow on old bread.

Uncovered food is contaminated by *mould* spores from the air.

motion   *noun*   حركة

Movement; changing position

Observe different animals in *motion* as they walk, swim and fly.

The particles of a gas are in constant *motion* – colliding with each other and the container walls.

muscle   *noun*   عضلة

A body part that powers movement

The biceps *muscle* bends the arm at the elbow.

A *muscle* can only pull, it cannot push

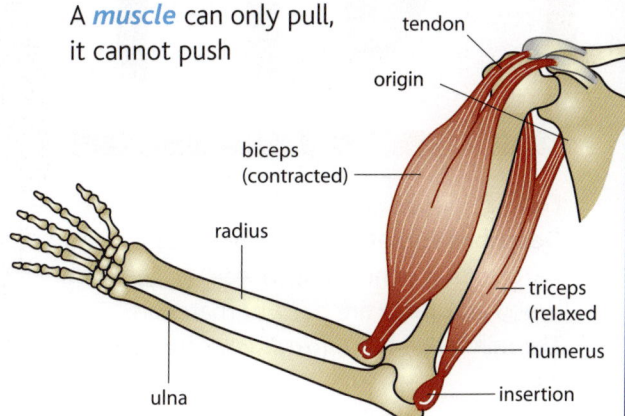

tendon
origin
biceps (contracted)
radius
triceps (relaxed
humerus
insertion
ulna

musical instrument

noun   آلة موسيقية

A sound source designed to make musical sounds

Violins, guitars, trumpets and drums are *musical instruments*.

Most *musical instruments* can be controlled to play a range of different notes.

Nn

natural   *adjective*   طبيعي
Describes something that occurs in nature; that is not man-made
Wood and stone are *natural* materials.
The rain forest is a *natural* environment.

natural disaster
noun   كارثة طبيعية
A destructive event caused by natural forces
Hurricanes, earthquakes, tsunamis, floods and volcanic eruptions are *natural disasters*.
Many people are killed or injured when a *natural disaster* strikes a major city.

negative   *adjective*   سالب
Describes one of the two types of electric charge
The current flows from the positive battery terminal to the *negative* terminal around the circuit.
An electron carries a *negative* electric charge.

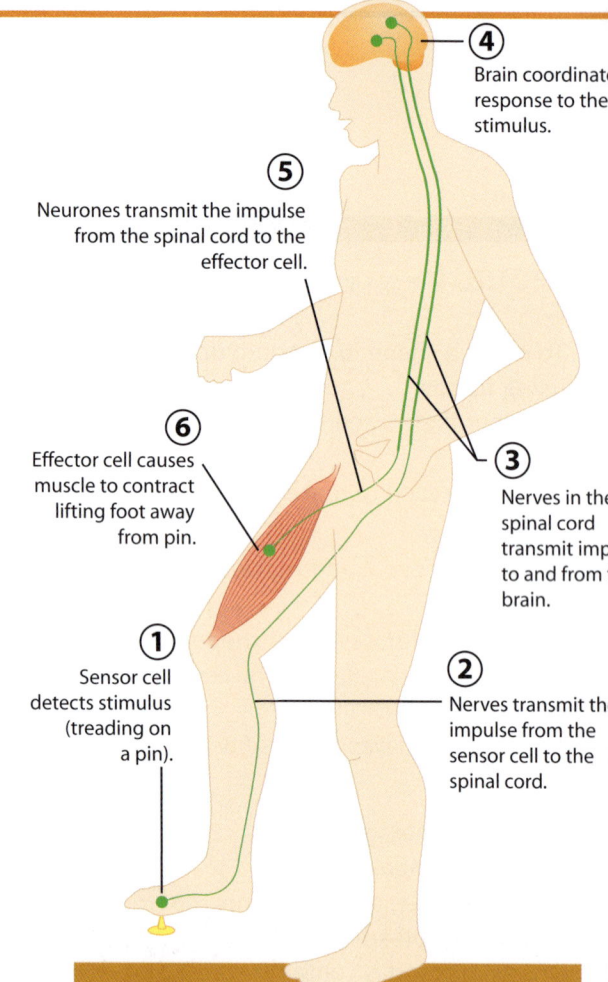

④ Brain coordinate response to the stimulus.

⑤ Neurones transmit the impulse from the spinal cord to the effector cell.

⑥ Effector cell causes muscle to contract lifting foot away from pin.

③ Nerves in the spinal cord transmit impu to and from t brain.

① Sensor cell detects stimulus (treading on a pin).

② Nerves transmit the impulse from the sensor cell to the spinal cord.

nerve   *noun*   عصب
A thin fibre that carries signals through the body
Information from the retina travels along the optic *nerve* to the brain.
Signals travel along a *nerve* as pulses of electric charge.

nervous system
noun   الجهاز العصبي
The brain and the network of nerves that control the body
An animal's senses provide information to its *nervous system*.
Plants do not have a *nervous system*.

neutron *noun* نيوترون

A particle in the nucleus of an atom

A *neutron* does not have an electric charge.
The nucleus of the carbon atom consists of
six protons and six *neutrons*.

nitrogen *noun* نيتروجين

The most common gas in the atmosphere

The atmosphere is approximately 79 per cent
nitrogen.
Nitrogen does not support combustion or
respiration.

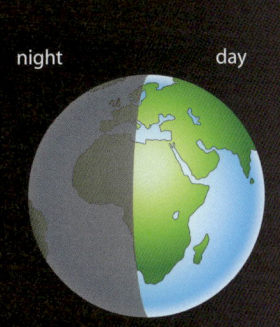

night   day

night *noun* ليل

**The period of darkness when the Sun is
below the horizon**

It is *night* on the side of the Earth facing
away from the Sun.
Most places on Earth experience one period
of daylight and one of *night* every 24 hours.

nocturnal *adjective* ليلي

Active at night

The owl is a *nocturnal* hunter.
Bats and other *nocturnal* animals often have
very good hearing.

non-living thing

non-living thing *noun*   جماد
Something that is not, and has never been, alive
A stone is a *non-living thing*.
A horse is alive – its leather saddle was once part of a living thing, but its metal shoes are *non-living things*.

non-renewable
adjective   غير متجدد
Describes energy sources and other resources that are not naturally replaced as they are used
The fossil fuels coal, oil and natural gas are *non-renewable* energy sources.
The more we use *non-renewable* resources, the sooner they will run out.

nose *noun*   أنف
The sense organ we use to detect smells
The *nose* warms and filters the air we breathe.
Smell sensors in the *nose* are sensitive to tiny amounts of substances in the air.

nucleus *noun*   نواة
The tiny, central part of an atom
Most of the mass of an atom is concentrated in its *nucleus*.
The *nucleus* is made up of protons and neutrons.

nutrient *noun*   مادة غذائية
A substance the body needs from food for growth, maintenance and repair
The five main types of *nutrients* are proteins, carbohydrates, fats, vitamins and minerals.
A balanced diet provides all the *nutrients* the body needs.

nutrition *noun*   تغذية
The process of obtaining energy and materials for life – by feeding, for example
Animals must eat plants or other animals for *nutrition*.
Plants obtain *nutrition* from sunlight through photosynthesis.

Oo

obesity *noun* بدانة

The condition of being very overweight

Obesity is linked to a higher risk of diabetes and heart disease.
The consumption of 'junk food' and lack of exercise are leading to increased rates of *obesity* around the world.

observation *noun* ملاحظة

The act of looking with interest and care to try to understand something

Record your *observations* in a notebook. You could use a magnifying glass to make more detailed *observations*.

omnivore
noun آكل الحيوان والنبات

An animal that eats a mixture of plant and animal food

Human beings and bears are *omnivores*.
In a food chain, an *omnivore* may be a primary or a secondary consumer.

opaque *adjective* معتم

Describes a material that does not allow light to pass through it

Polished metal is *opaque* because it reflects light that falls on it.
Black cloth is *opaque* because it absorbs incident light.

optical instrument
noun جهاز بصري

An instrument that uses lenses, mirrors or prisms to bend and focus light to make images

Spectacles are *optical instruments* designed to correct poor vision.
Optical instruments such as the periscope, telescope, microscope, projector and camera help us view the world more clearly, and create images with light.

a b c d e f g h i j k l m n o p q r s t u v w x y z

orbit

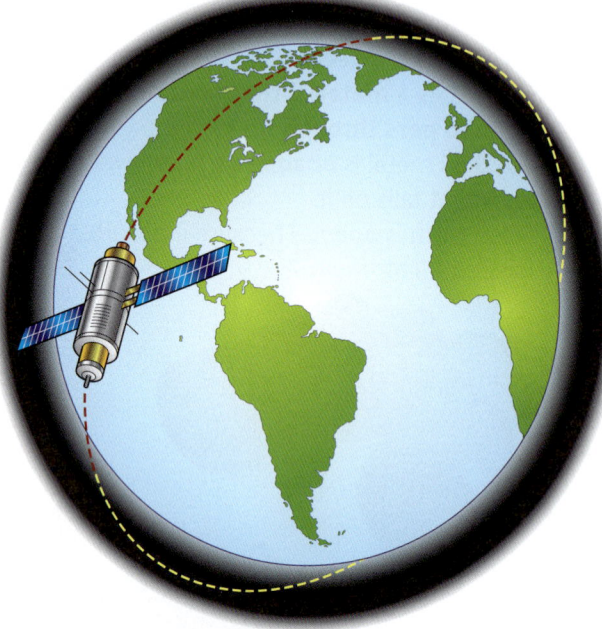

orbit *noun*
مدار

The circular or elliptical path that an object in space follows around a larger object

The eight planets of the solar system are held in their *orbit* by the force of gravity.
A rocket places a communications satellite into *orbit* around the Earth.

organ *noun*
عضو (في الجسم)

A body part with a particular job to do

The brain and the heart are major body *organs*.
An insect's antennae are sense *organs* for detecting smell.

organism *noun*
كائن حي

A living thing

Pond water is full of microscopic *organisms*.
A parasite is a living thing that lives on, or in, the body of another *organism*.

organ system *noun*
جهاز عضوي وظيفي

A group of organs that work together to perform a complex task such as respiration or excretion

The stomach and intestines are organs of the digestive *organ system*.
The skeletal *organ system* gives your body shape and protects internal organs.

oscillation *noun*
تذبذب

Repeated to and fro movement

The *oscillation* of a pendulum can control the timing of a clock.
Rapid *oscillation* is also described as 'vibration'.

ozone layer

ovary *noun*   مِبيَض
An organ that produces or holds female reproductive cells
A female animal's *ovaries* produce ova (egg cells).
A flower's *ovary* holds the ovules.

ovule *noun*   بويضة (نباتات)
The female reproductive cell of a plant and the parts that contain it
A tube grows from the pollen grain, down the style, to an *ovule* in the ovary.
Following fertilisation, the ovary and the *ovules* become the fruit and the seeds.

ovum *noun*   بويضة
A female reproductive cell
The human *ovum* is one of the largest cells in the body.
During ovulation, an *ovum* is released from the ovary into the fallopian tube.

oxygen *noun*   أكسجين
The second most common gas in the atmosphere
Oxygen is the gas we must breathe to stay alive.
A fire can be extinguished by preventing *oxygen* from reaching the flames.

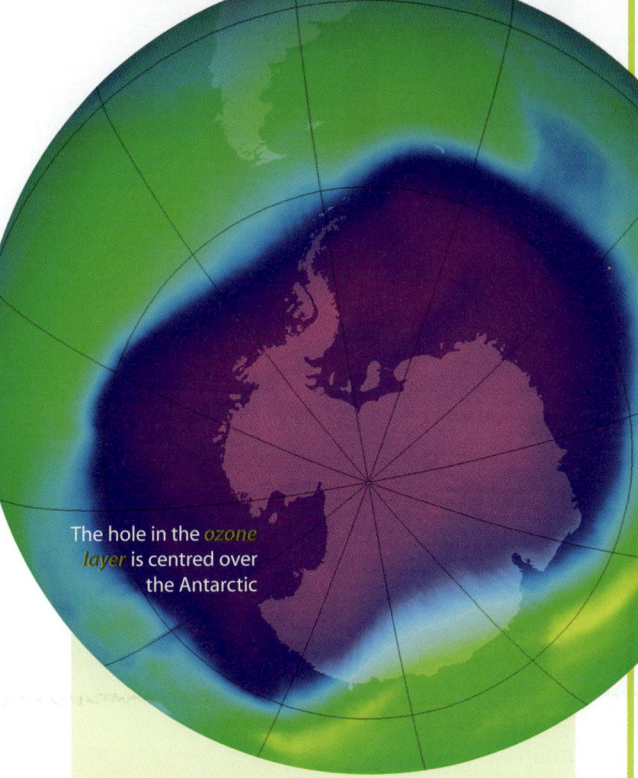

The hole in the *ozone layer* is centred over the Antarctic

ozone *noun*   أوزون
A special kind of oxygen gas
Normal oxygen has two oxygen atoms in each molecule; *ozone* has three.
Ozone may be produced from normal oxygen by high voltage electric sparks, lightning, and UV light.

ozone layer *noun*   طبقة الأوزون
A layer of ozone gas high in the atmosphere
The *ozone layer* absorbs harmful UV rays from the Sun.
Pollution by man-made chemicals called CFCs has made a hole in the *ozone layer*.

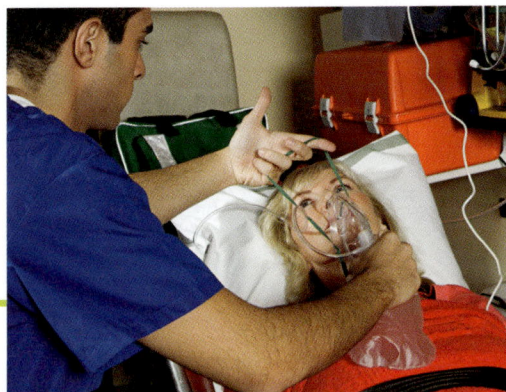

P p

pandemic *noun* وباء

An epidemic that spreads across international borders

International travel makes it difficult to control flu *pandemics*.
In the 19th century, cholera *pandemics* killed millions of people.

parallel circuit *noun* دائرة موصّلة على التوازي

An electric circuit with two or more paths (branches) that the current can take

In a *parallel circuit*, the current divides as it flows through the different branches.
If one bulb in a *parallel circuit* fails, the other bulbs stay lit.

parasite *noun* طفيل

An organism that lives on another organism, causing it harm

The organism on which a *parasite* lives is called its host.
Fleas are *parasites* that live on mammals and birds.

particle *noun* جسيم / جزيء

A small, individual piece of matter

Each grain of sand is a separate *particle*.
An atom is the smallest *particle* of an element.

penumbra *noun* شبه ظل

The outer, partial shadow produced by an extended (large) light source

The *penumbra* is not as dark as the umbra.
An observer in the *penumbra* of the Moon's shadow sees a partial eclipse.

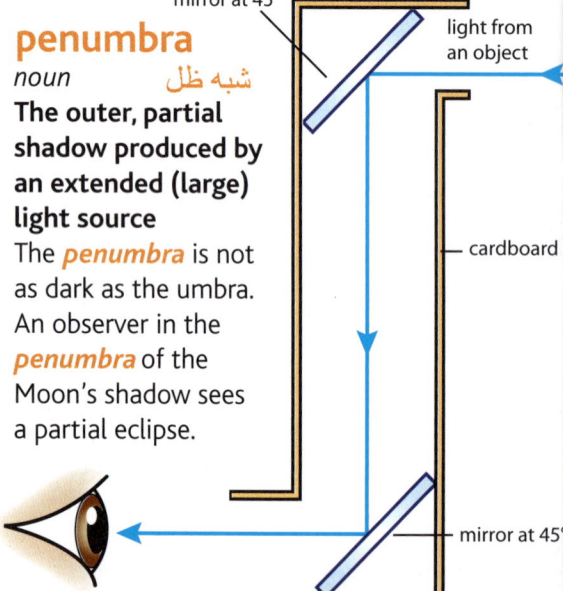

mirror at 45°
light from an object
cardboard
mirror at 45°

periscope *noun* البريسكوب / منظار الأفق

An optical instrument for seeing over barriers or around corners

A submarine captain uses a *periscope* to see above the water surface.
You can make a simple *periscope* by placing two mirrors at angles of 45° at either end of a tube.

permanent change *noun* تغير دائم

A change that cannot easily be reversed

Combustion is a chemical reaction; it is a *permanent change*.
Changes of state such as melting and boiling are not *permanent changes*.

photosynthesis

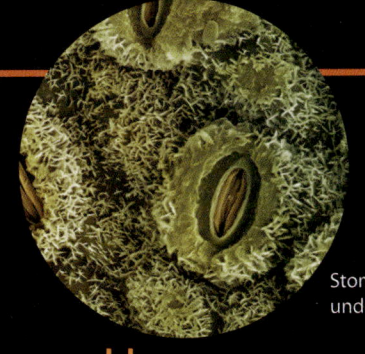

Stomata on the underside of a leaf

permeable *adjective* منفَّذ

Describes a substance through which another substance may pass
Cotton cloth is *permeable* to water. Pores called stomata in the underside of a leaf make it *permeable* to water vapour and other gases.

petal *noun* بتلة

One of the brightly coloured parts of a flower
The flower's *petals* are arranged in a ring. Coloured *petals* attract insects and birds to the flower.

pH
noun درجة الحموضة / الأس الهيدروجيني

A scale that measures the strength of acids and alkalis; also the measure of how acidic or basic something is
The *pH* of pure water is 7.
The *pH* of an acid is less than 7; the *pH* of an alkali is greater than 7.

14	liquid drain cleaner, caustic soda
13	bleach
12	soapy water
11	household ammonia
10	milk of magnesium
9	toothpaste
8	seawater, eggs
7	'pure' water
6	milk
5	black coffee
4	tomato juice
3	grapefruit & orange juice
2	lemon juice, vinegar
1	hydrochloric acid
0	battery acid

examples of solutions and their respective pH

phases of the Moon
noun أطوار القمر

The changing appearance of the Moon over a period of 29.5 days
New, crescent, gibbous and Full Moon are different *phases of the Moon*.
In the Islamic calendar, a new month begins with the *phase of the Moon* called the Hilal – the first Crescent Moon after a New Moon.

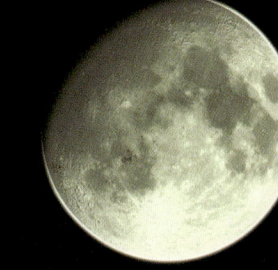

photosynthesis
noun عملية البناء الضوئي

The processes by which plants capture the energy of sunlight for nutrition
Photosynthesis takes place in the green parts of the plant – mainly the leaves.
In *photosynthesis*, carbon dioxide and water are combined to make glucose and oxygen.

pinhole camera

pinhole camera

noun　　　　　　　كاميرا ذات ثقب

A box with a pinhole through which light rays pass to form an image on a screen

The *pinhole camera* was invented by Ibn al-Haytham (Alhazen) more than 1000 years ago.

Alhazen discovered that the smaller the hole in the *pinhole camera*, the clearer the image.

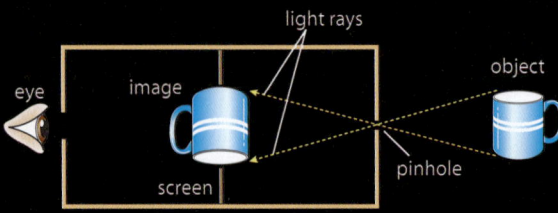

eye · image · light rays · object · pinhole · screen

pitch (sound)

noun　　　　درجة النغمة / طبقة الصوت

The position of a sound on a scale from low to high

A small bird sings at a high *pitch*.

To change the *pitch* of the notes from a flute, you cover and uncover the finger holes.

planet *noun*　　　كوكب

A huge ball of matter that orbits a star

There are eight *planets* in our solar system. Astronomers have discovered many *planets* orbiting other stars.

plant *noun*　　نبات

A member of the plant kingdom of living things

All *plants* have these characteristics:

- *plants* are made from many tiny cells
- *plants* use the substance cellulose to give their bodies shape and strength
- *plants* obtain nutrition by photosynthesis, and usually store food as starch or sucrose (a kind of sugar)

Almost every food chain begins with a *plant*. In an ecosystem, the *plants* are the producers.

pole (magnetism) *noun*　　قطب

The part of a magnet where the magnetic force is strongest

Every magnet has two *poles*: a north pole and a south pole.

The laws of magnetism are that like *poles* repel; unlike poles attract.

pollen *noun*　　حبوب اللقاح

Tiny male particles made by a flower to fertilise the female parts

Pollen is produced by the flower's anthers. Hay fever is an allergic reaction to *pollen* in the air.

pollination *noun*　　تلقيح

The process of transferring pollen from anthers to female flower parts

The *pollination* of grasses and many trees is caused by the wind. Insects, birds and bats are agents for the *pollination* of colourful flowers.

prey

pollution
noun   تلوث

Harmful waste or energy released into the environment

The *pollution* of water with human waste spreads disease.

Sound *pollution* is a problem near major airports.

positive   adjective   موجب

Describes one of the two types of electric charge

The protons in an atomic nucleus carry a *positive* charge.

Connect the shorter wire to the *positive* terminal.

potential energy
noun   طاقة كامنة

The energy something has because of its position or state

A mass raised above the ground has gravitational *potential energy*.

A stretched rubber band stores elastic *potential energy*.

power supply
noun   مصدر الطاقة (الكهرباء)

A source of electrical energy

In this circuit, the battery is the *power supply*.

You must disconnect the *power supply* before removing the cover from an electrical appliance.

predator   noun   حيوان مفترس

An animal that hunts other animals for food

Sharks are marine *predators*.

A *predator* may be camouflaged to help it stalk its prey.

prediction   noun   تنبؤ

A suggestion for the likely outcome of an experiment or observation

Use your scientific knowledge to make a *prediction* of the result.

A good theory makes *predictions* that can be tested with experiments.

pressure   noun   ضغط

Force acting over an area

A gas exerts *pressure* on the walls of its container.

Falling air *pressure* indicates that the weather conditions may become worse.

prey   noun   فريسة

An animal that is hunted by other animals

An eagle is a predator; a rabbit is its *prey*.

Prey animals may gather in flocks to gain protection from predators.

primary consumer

primary consumer

noun مُستهلك أوّلي

An animal in a food chain that feeds directly on plants

Antelopes and other grazing animals are the *primary consumers* on the grasslands. *Primary consumers* are generally more numerous than the secondary consumers that prey on them.

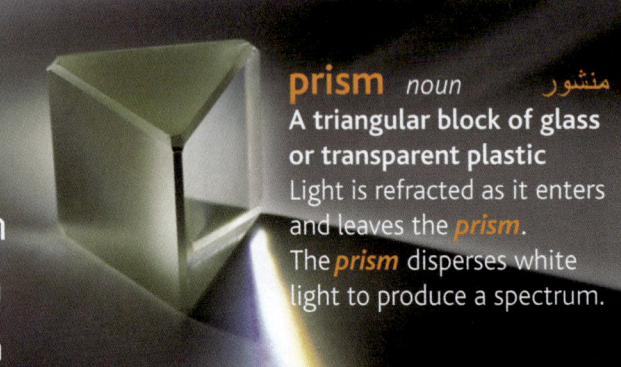

prism *noun* منشور

A triangular block of glass or transparent plastic

Light is refracted as it enters and leaves the *prism*. The *prism* disperses white light to produce a spectrum.

producer *noun* منتج

A plant in an ecosystem

Plants are described as *producers* because they produce (make) their own food through photosynthesis.

Without plants to act as *producers*, there could be no consumers (animals).

property *noun* خاصية

A feature or characteristic of something

Properties such as strength and flexibility are important when select ing materials for construction. Density is the *property* that determines if a material floats or sinks.

protein *noun* بروتين

The nutrient we need from our food for growth and repair of the body

Fish, meat, dairy products, nuts and pulses are good sources of *protein*.

A shortage of *protein* in the diet causes the deficiency disease kwashiorkor.

protist

noun حيوان اولي

A type of microscopic organism with one or more cells

Amoeba and the plasmodium parasites that cause malaria are members of the *protist* kingdom of living things. *Protist* cells have nuclei; monera cells do not have nuclei.

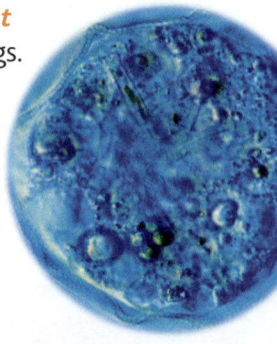

proton

noun بروتون

A particle in the nucleus of an atom

A *proton* has a positive electric charge. The number of *protons* in the nucleus is the atomic number; different elements have different atomic numbers.

puberty *noun* مرحلة البلوغ

The changes that take place when the body matures and becomes capable of reproduction

Boys and girls experience a growth spurt at *puberty*.

For a girl, *puberty* may normally start from age 10 onwards; for boys, *puberty* usually begins 1–2 years later.

pull
verb يجذب / يشد

To apply a force that tries to move objects together

Pull the rope to drag the weight towards you. The force of gravity *pulls* objects to the ground.

pulley
noun بكرة

A grooved wheel over which a rope or belt runs

A *pulley* is a simple machine that changes the direction of a force. *Pulleys* can be combined to raise a large load with a smaller effort.

pulse *noun* نبض

The regular throb of flowing blood

You can feel your *pulse* on your wrist, where an artery is close to the surface.

Your *pulse* is caused by the rise and fall of your blood pressure as the heart beats.

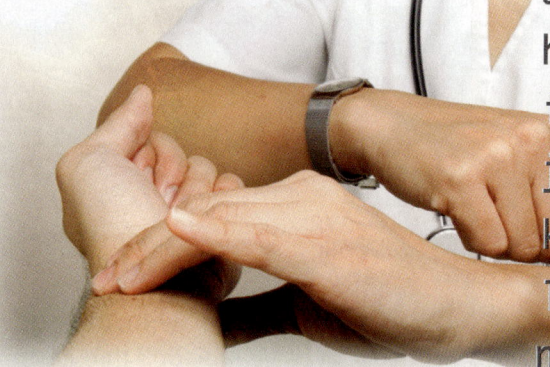

pump
noun مضخة

A device for making fluids flow

The heart is a *pump*.
A bicycle *pump* forces air into a tyre to raise its pressure.

pupil *noun* البؤبؤ

The black dot at the centre of the eye

Light enters the eye through the *pupil*.
In dim light, the iris makes the *pupil* larger to allow more light into the eye.

push *verb* يدفع

To apply a force that tries to move objects away or apart

Push the truck to start it moving.
The north pole of one magnet *pushes* the north pole of a second magnet away – like poles repel.

Rr

radiation *noun* — إشعاع
One of the ways in which heat travels
Heat travels by *radiation* through empty space from the Sun to the Earth.
The heat *radiation* from a red hot fire warms your skin.

rainbow *noun* — قوس قزح
An arc of different light colours in the sky
The colours of the *rainbow* are dispersed (separated) as sunlight is refracted by raindrops.
The scientific word for the *rainbow* pattern produced when a mixture of light colours is dispersed is 'spectrum'.

rain forest *noun* — غابات مطيرة
A tropical forest with tall trees, dense foliage and high rainfall
The *rain forest* has more species of plants and animals than any other ecosystem.
Rain forests are threatened with destruction through human actions.

ray *noun* — شعاع
A straight arrow that shows the direction in which light is travelling
A *ray* is a straight line because light travels in straight lines.
Draw *rays* to show how light is reflected from a mirror.

reaction *noun* — تفاعل
A chemical change when two or more substances combine to make new substances
The *reaction* between vinegar and baking soda produces the gas carbon dioxide.
Some chemical *reactions* give out heat, others absorb heat.

reproduction

record *verb*
يسجل

To note something permanently by writing it down, drawing or photographing it, or by entering it into a computer
Good scientists *record* all their observations and measurements.
Record your measurements in a table.

recycle
يعيد استخدام / يدوّر
verb

To reclaim materials from waste to be used again
Waste paper, metal and glass can be *recycled* to manufacture new products.
Recycling helps the environment by saving energy and reducing waste dumping.

refraction
noun
انكسار

The change in direction of light as it travels from one medium to another
Refraction causes a spoon standing in a glass of water to appear bent.
Refraction at the surface of the lens makes parallel rays converge.

renewable *adjective*
متجدد

Describes an energy source that is constantly replaced – it does not get used up
Solar, wind and wave energy are *renewable* energy sources.
To combat global warming, we must replace fossil fuels with *renewable* energy sources.

repel *verb*
يتنافر

To push away or apart
Like charges *repel*.
The force of gravity only attracts, it does not *repel*.

reproduction
noun
تكاثر

The process of producing offspring (young)
In sexual *reproduction*, special cells from a male and a female combine.
Puberty is the life stage during which human beings become capable of *reproduction*.

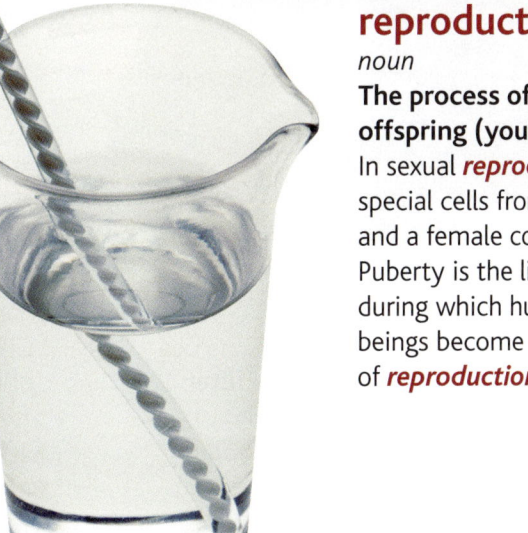

a b c d e f g h i j k l m n o p q **r** s t u v w x y z

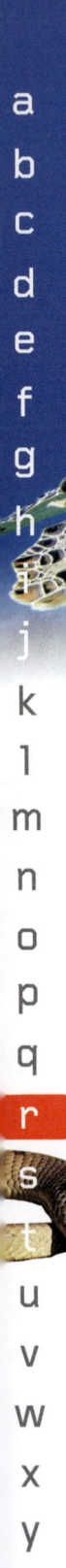

reptile

bronchus

trachea

bronchiole

rib muscle

rib

alveoli

heart

lungs

diaphragm

reptile *noun* زواحف
A cold-blooded vertebrate animal that reproduces on land
Lizards, crocodiles, snakes and turtles are *reptiles*.
Most *reptiles* reproduce by laying eggs.

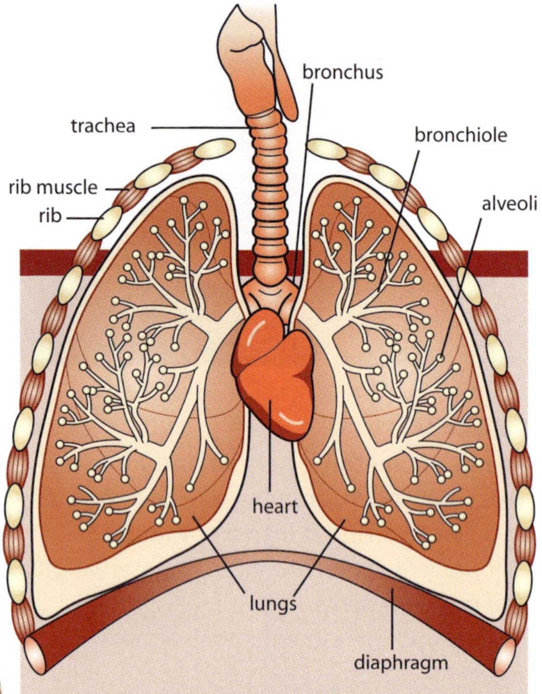

respiration *noun* تنفس
The process of breathing in and out to obtain oxygen and excrete waste gases; also the release of energy from food in cells
During *respiration*, oxygen passes through the lung walls into the blood.
Respiration takes place in body cells when glucose from digested food combines with oxygen from the blood.

respiratory system
noun جهاز التنفس
The organ system that transfers oxygen from air (or water, for aquatic animals) into the body
The lungs are the main organ of the human *respiratory system*.
Gills are organs of the *respiratory system* of fish and other aquatic animals.

residue *noun* بقايا
The solid particles trapped by the filter paper during filtration
Filter the mixture and collect the *residue*.
Allow the *residue* to dry, and then weigh it.

76

rotation

reversible change

noun تغير عكسي

A physical change to a material, which can easily be reversed (undone)

Melting, boiling and other changes of state are *reversible changes*.

A *reversible change* can be undone by reversing the conditions that caused it – cooling instead of heating, for example.

Magnitude	Description	Effects
1	Micro	Not felt
2	Very minor	Usually not felt but can be recorded
3	Minor	Often felt – but rarely cause damage
4	Light	Plates and cups rattle, but significant damage unlikely
5	Moderate	Major damage to poorly constructed buildings
6	Strong	May cause major damage in an area up to 100 miles across

Richter scale *noun* مقياس ريختر

A scale of the strengths of earthquakes

The 2011 earthquake in Japan was magnitude 9 on the *Richter scale*.

An earthquake of magnitude 4 on the *Richter scale* makes plates and cups rattle but does not do significant damage.

rock *noun* صخرة

A natural solid made from one or more minerals

The Earth's crust is made from *rock*. Granite is a hard igneous *rock*.

root *noun* جذر

One of the parts of a plant that usually grows down to anchor it in the soil

Plants absorb water and minerals through their *roots*. Some plants store food in their *roots* – the carrot, for example.

rotation *noun* دوران

Turning or spinning motion

The *rotation* of the Earth on its axis gives us day and night.

The crankshaft in an engine changes the up and down motion of the pistons into *rotation*.

Ss

salt *noun* ملح
A chemical compound made by the reaction between an acid and a metal or a base
'Sodium chloride' is the chemical name for common *salt*.
The reaction between copper oxide and sulphuric acid produces the *salt* copper sulphate.

sand *noun* رمل
A natural material composed of grains of rock up to 2 mm in diameter
Wind and water transport *sand* particles to form beaches and dunes.
A *sandy (adjective)* soil is light in colour, feels gritty and drains quickly.

scale
noun مقياس مدرّج
A regular set of marks or divisions against which a measurement is made
The ruler *scale* is marked in millimetres and centimetres.
On the Celsius *scale*, the boiling point of water is 100°C.

screw *noun* بُرغي/مسمار لولبي
A simple machine with a spiral thread
One full turn moves the *screw* forward by just one pitch of the thread.
The force used to turn a *screw* is concentrated to produce a much greater force along its length.

season *noun* موسم
A time of the year marked by the weather
Summer is the hottest *season* of the year.
Temperate climates have four *seasons*: summer, autumn, winter and spring.

second *noun* ثانِية
The scientific unit of time
Your heart beats approximately once each *second*.
There are 60 *seconds* in 1 minute and 60 minutes in 1 hour.

secondary consumer
noun مستهلك ثانوي
An animal that obtains its nutrition by eating animals that eat plants
Lions are *secondary consumers* because they eat grazing animals such as zebras.
There is less food available to *secondary consumers* than to primary consumers because energy is lost at each stage of a food chain.

sedimentary *adjective* ترسيب
Describes rocks formed from layers of mud and sand that settled at the bottom of the sea
Chalk and sandstone are *sedimentary* rocks.
Sedimentary rocks are generally soft and light in colour.

seed *noun* بذور

The small product of plant sexual reproduction, which may germinate to produce a new plant

Following fertilisation, the ovum develops into a *seed*.

In order to germinate, the *seed* requires moisture and warmth.

sense *noun* الإحساس/الحاسّة

A way in which a living thing obtains information about its surroundings

Human beings have five *senses*: sight, hearing, smell, taste and touch.

A dog's *sense* of smell is far more sensitive than a human's.

sense organ *noun* عضو حِسّي

A body organ that responds to a particular type of stimulus to create one of the senses

The eyes, ears, tongue, nose and skin are our *sense organs*.

An insect's antennae are *sense organs*; they detect molecules in the air.

separation *noun* فصل

The process of taking apart things that have been mixed

Magnetic *separation* can be used to separate steel cans from aluminium cans.

Filtration is a *separation* method used to separate solid particles from a liquid.

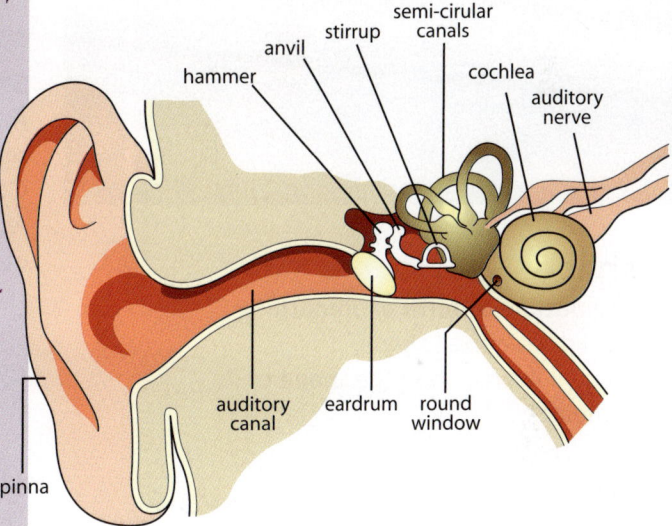

semi-cirular canals · stirrup · anvil · hammer · cochlea · auditory nerve · auditory canal · eardrum · round window · pinna

series circuit

noun دائرة موصلة على التوالي

An electric circuit in which the components are connected in a single loop, one after the other

The current in a *series circuit* flows through each component in turn.

If one bulb in a *series circuit* blows, the current stops flowing and all the other bulbs go out.

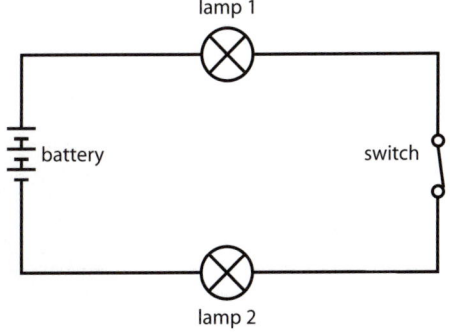

lamp 1 · battery · switch · lamp 2

shadow

shadow *noun* ظل
A dark region from which light has been blocked by an object
An opaque object casts a *shadow* because light travels in straight lines.
Light from the light source cannot reach the *shadow* region on the far side of the object.

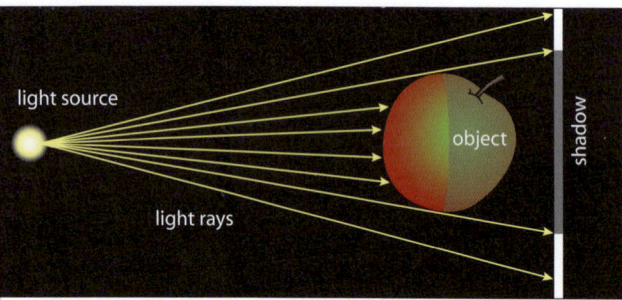

shape *noun* شكل
The outline or form of something
A solid has a fixed *shape*.
A liquid flows to take the *shape* of its container.

sieve *noun* منخل/مصفاة
A wire grid for separating particles by size (sieving)
You can use a *sieve* to separate grains of rice from flour.
A garden *sieve* allows small stones to pass through, but traps larger stones.

sink *verb* يغوص
To drop beneath the surface of water
Stones, and other objects that are heavy for their size, *sink* in water.
An object *sinks* when the upthrust from the water is not great enough to balance its weight.

skeleton *noun* هيكل عظمي
The hard parts of an animal that give its body shape and protection
An adult human *skeleton* consists of 206 bones.
Vertebrate animals have an internal *skeleton*; insects and other arthropods have an external *skeleton*.

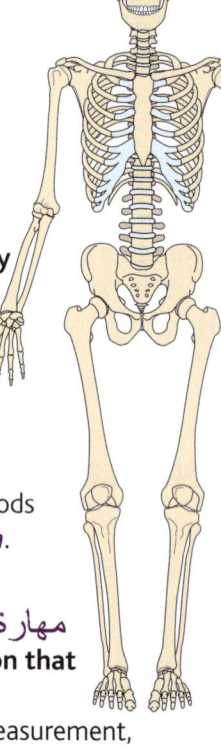

skill *noun* مهارة
A special ability or action that requires training
Observation, planning, measurement, recording and data handling are just some of the *skills* you will develop as you study science.
The accurate use of instruments such as stop watches, tape measures and thermometers is a *skill* you must practise.

skin *noun* جلد
The thin surface layer of the body
The *skin* is a hard-wearing, waterproof and germ-proof layer that protects the body.
The evaporation of sweat from the *skin* helps control body temperature.

soil *noun* تربة
The crumbly top layer of the ground, in which plants grow
Soil is a mixture of rock particles of different sizes, living things and humus (rotted organic material).
Sandy, clay and loam are the three main *soil* types.

solvent

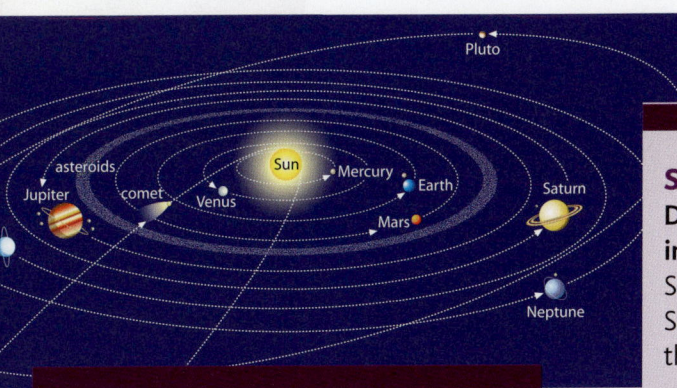

soluble *adjective* قابل للذوبان
Describes a substance that dissolves in a liquid
Salt and sugar are *soluble* in water.
Sugar is more *soluble* in warm water than in cold water.

solar *adjective* شمسي
Describes something related to the Sun
A *solar* cell converts the energy of sunlight into electrical energy.
Solar energy is a renewable, non-polluting energy source.

solute *noun* مُذاب
A substance which is dissolved in a liquid
Stir the mixture until all the *solute* has dissolved.
You can separate the *solute* from a solution by allowing the solvent to evaporate.

solar system
noun المجموعة الشمسية
Our Sun, its eight planets, their moons and all the other objects held in our part of space by the Sun's gravity
The planets in our *solar system* are Mercury, Venus, Earth, Mars, Jupiter, Saturn, Uranus and Neptune.
Our *solar system* formed from gas and dust in space about 5 billion years ago.

solution *noun* محلول
A mixture in which the atoms or molecules of one substance are separated and spread out between those of another substance
A *solution* is a homogeneous mixture.
A *solution* cannot be separated by filtration.

solid *noun* صلب
The state of matter, or a substance, in which the particles are packed closely together in fixed positions
A *solid* has a fixed shape.
The particles in a *solid* are held in place by strong bonds between neighbours.

solvent *noun* مذيب
The liquid into which another substance dissolves
When you dissolve sugar in water, the water is the *solvent*.
You can remove a stain with a suitable *solvent*.

81

sound

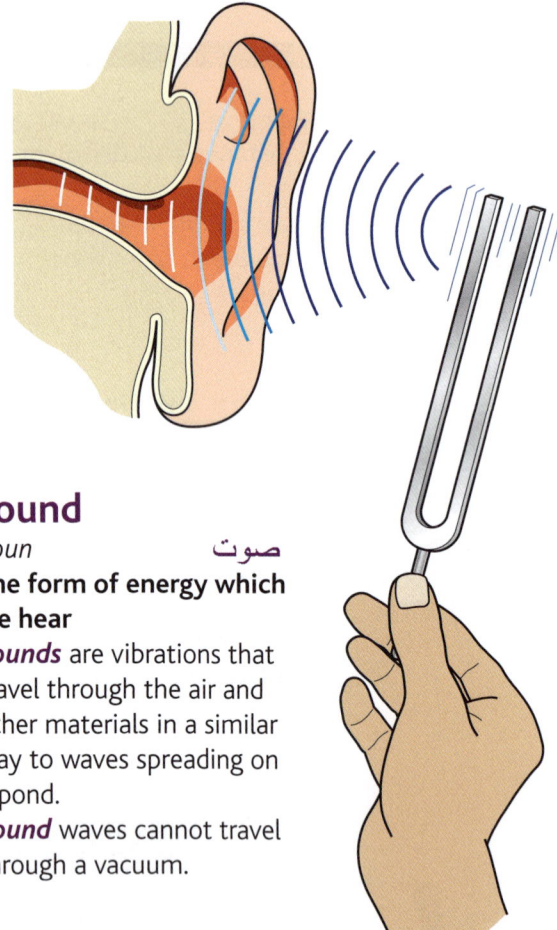

spectrum

noun طيف

The band of different colours seen when a mixture of light colours is dispersed

Isaac Newton used a glass prism to create the *spectrum* of sunlight.

A rainbow is a natural *spectrum* produced by raindrops.

speed *noun* سرعة

The measure of how fast something moves; the rate of covering distance

The *speed* of a car is measured in kilometres per hour (kph) or miles per hour (mph).

We calculate *speed* by dividing the distance travelled by the time taken.

sound

noun صوت

The form of energy which we hear

Sounds are vibrations that travel through the air and other materials in a similar way to waves spreading on a pond.

Sound waves cannot travel through a vacuum.

space *noun* فراغ

The emptiness between things; the volume or extent which things occupy

Matter has mass and takes up *space*.

Space has three dimensions.

species *noun* أنواع (كائنات حية)

A group of all the living things of the same type

Members of a *species* share the same characteristics and can breed with each other.

Lions, tigers, leopards and jaguars are different *species* of cats.

spring *noun* زنبرك

A wire spiral that springs back to shape if it is compressed or stretched

A weight suspended from a *spring* oscillates up and down.

The extension of the *spring* is proportional to the load.

spring *noun* الربيع

The season between winter and summer

During *spring*, the weather gradually gets warmer.

Spring is the time of year when many animals produce young.

stamen

noun السداة (عضو التذكير في الزهرة)

A male part of a flower

The *stamen* consists of the filament and the anther.

A ring of *stamens* surround the carpel.

star *noun* نجم

A vast glowing sphere of matter in space that gives out enormous quantities of energy

The Sun is our nearest *star*.

All the *stars*, apart from the Sun, are so far away they appear as tiny points of light.

steam *noun* بخار

Water in the gas state

Water changes state from liquid to *steam* at 100°C.

When it touches a cold surface, the *steam* from a boiling kettle condenses to drops of liquid water.

stem *noun* ساق

The main part of a plant that usually grows above the ground

The *stem* supports the branches, leaves and flowers.

The *stem* transports water and minerals from the roots to the rest of the plant.

stigma

noun ميسم: الجزء الأعلى من مدقة الزّهرة

A female part of the flower, which receives pollen

The *stigma* is at the top of the carpel.

Pollination takes place when pollen is transferred to the *stigma*.

strength *noun* قوة

The measure of how much force or weight something can support without breaking

Strength is an important property when selecting the material to build a bridge.

A triangular structure has more *strength* than a square one.

style

style

noun   قلم:الجزء الحامل للميسم في الزهرة

The stalk that supports the stigma in a flower

The *style* sits on top of the ovary with the stigma at its tip.

Following pollination, a pollen tube grows down the inside of the *style* to the ovary.

substance   noun   مادة

A particular material or type of matter

Water is the most common *substance* in the human body.

Which *substance* is inflammable – rubber, wax, wood, stone, oil or plastic?

substance abuse

noun   إساءة استخدام مادة

The use of drugs, solvents or other substances that cause physical or mental harm

Inhaling solvents is a dangerous form of *substance abuse* that can cause sudden death.

Substance abuse may lead to addiction.

Sun   noun   الشمس

The star at the centre of our solar system

Light from the *Sun* takes 8 minutes to reach the Earth.

You must never look directly at the *Sun*; it will damage your eyes.

support   verb   يدعم

To hold up

The stem *supports* the branches and the leaves.

The skeleton *supports* the body and gives it shape.

suspension

noun   معلق

A mixture in which fine solid particles are mixed throughout a liquid

A *suspension* has a cloudy appearance.

Solid particles can be separated from a *suspension* by filtration.

switch   noun   مفتاح

A circuit component that turns an electric current on or off

When the *switch* is in the off position it creates a break in the circuit.

Turning the *switch* on completes the circuit so the current can flow.

Tt

table *noun*   جدول
A chart that groups data in rows and columns
Record your readings of temperature and time in a suitable *table*.
In the periodic *table*, elements with similar properties appear in the same column.

telescope *noun*   تليسكوب
An instrument for making distant objects appear closer
You can make a simple *telescope* with two lenses – the objective lens and the eyepiece lens.
Inside the Hubble space *telescope*, light from the stars is focused by a 2.4-metre diameter concave mirror.

temperate *adjective*   معتدل
Describes a climate that is neither extremely hot in summer nor extremely cold in winter
North-West Europe has a cool *temperate* climate; the weather is changeable and it can rain at any time of year.
In a *temperate* climate, the summer and winter seasons are about the same length.

temperature *noun*   درجة الحرارة
The measure of how hot or cold something is
Heat always flows from a higher temperature to a lower *temperature*.
The student used a thermometer to measure the *temperature* in degrees Celsius.

terrestrial *adjective*   أرضي
Describes something linked to the land rather than the sea or the air; also something to do with the Earth rather than space
The elephant is the largest *terrestrial* animal.
You need an antenna to receive *terrestrial* television transmissions.

test
verb   اختبار
To carry out a procedure to obtain information or to check an idea
Test the cans with a magnet to see which are steel cans.
Design an experiment to *test* a theory.

texture

texture _noun_ بُنية/صفة حسيّة

The feel of something when you touch or chew it

Feel the _texture_ of the fabrics – are they rough or smooth?

Compare the _texture_ of different fruits as you bite into them: are they soft, crisp, stringy or juicy?

theory _noun_ نظرية

A scientific explanation of observed facts

In science, _theories_ are based on evidence. A good _theory_ makes predictions that can be tested with experiments.

thermal _adjective_ حراري

Describes anything to do with heat or heat insulation

Arctic explorers wear several layers of _thermal_ clothing to keep warm.

Greenhouse gases trap _thermal_ energy in the Earth's atmosphere.

thermal _noun_ حرارة

A rising column of warm air in the atmosphere

On a hot day, _thermals_ rise from tarmac roads and other hot surfaces.

Vultures and eagles soar on _thermals_, gaining height without moving their wings.

thermometer _noun_ ترمومتر

An instrument for measuring temperature

A _thermometer_ scale is marked in degrees. A digital _thermometer_ records the temperature at the tip of the probe.

tide

noun المد والجزر

The twice daily rise and fall of the ocean

Tides are caused by the force of gravity from the Moon and the Sun.

The height difference between high and low _tides_ on some Atlantic coastlines can be up to 11 metres.

transparent

tissue *noun* نسيج

Body or plant material made from cells of one type

The heart is composed mainly of muscle *tissue*.

Individual nerve cells (neurons, or neurones) group together as nervous *tissue*.

tongue *noun* لسان

The muscular organ in the mouth

The surface of the *tongue* is covered with taste buds.

We use our *tongue* for tasting and swallowing, and also for forming the sounds of speech.

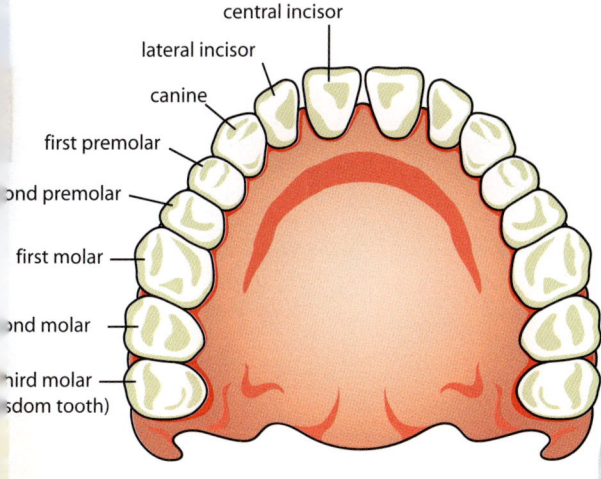

central incisor
lateral incisor
canine
first premolar
ond premolar
first molar
ond molar
hird molar
sdom tooth)

tooth *noun* سن/ضرس

The hard, sharp parts in the mouth which animals use to bite

Humans have two sets of *teeth* in their lifetime.

There are 32 *teeth* in a full adult set: 8 incisors, 4 canines, 8 premolars and 12 molars.

translation *noun* إزاحة/انتقال

Movement in a straight line

Translation takes an object from one place to another without rotation.

The movement of a train along a straight track is an example of *translation*.

translucent

adjective شبه شفّاف

Describes a material such as frosted glass that allows light through, but which you cannot see through clearly

Milk and tissue paper are *translucent*. Because light is scattered as it passes through a *translucent* material, you cannot see a clear image.

transparent

adjective شفّاف

Describes a material that allows light to pass through it in straight lines

Clear glass and water are *transparent*. A lens is made from a *transparent* material.

a
b
c
d
e
f
g
h
i
j
k
l
m
n
o
p
q
r
s
t
u
v
w
x
y
z

transport

transport *verb*

ينقل

To move or carry something

Vehicles *transport* people and goods from place to place.

The circulatory system *transports* nutrients and waste around the body.

tropical *adjective*

استوائي

Describes anything to do with the regions on either side of the Equator – the 'Tropics'

A *tropical* climate has a temperature of at least 18°C throughout the year.

In a *tropical* rain forest, the humidity is always high.

tsunami *noun*

تسونامي

A giant wave created by an undersea earthquake

In 2004, a *tsunami* in the Indian Ocean created one of the greatest natural disasters in history.

When there is a *tsunami* warning you must retreat from the coast to high ground.

turbine *noun*

توربين/محرك ذو دولاب

A machine that produces rotation from the force of moving water, the wind or high pressure steam

At a power station, *turbines* turn the generators to produce electricity.

A wind *turbine* has giant blades like a propeller to catch the energy of the wind.

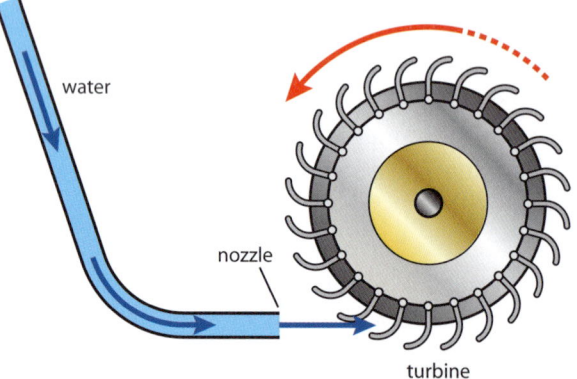

water

nozzle

turbine

Uu

umbra *noun*   ظل

The dark centre of a shadow

Light is completely blocked from the *umbra* of a shadow.

When you observe a total solar eclipse you are standing in the *umbra* of the Moon's shadow.

uncertainty *noun*   شك

The state when something is not known for sure or with 100 per cent accuracy

There is still *uncertainty* about the origin of life.

You can reduce the *uncertainty* in measurements by repeating them and taking an average.

unit *noun*   وحدة

A basic interval or amount used to make a measurement scale

The *units* on the tape measure are millimetres (mm) and centimetres.

The second is a small *unit* of time.

Universe *noun*   الكون

The whole of space and everything in it; everything that exists

The *Universe* is still expanding from the Big Bang.

Our galaxy is just one of billions of galaxies in the *Universe*.

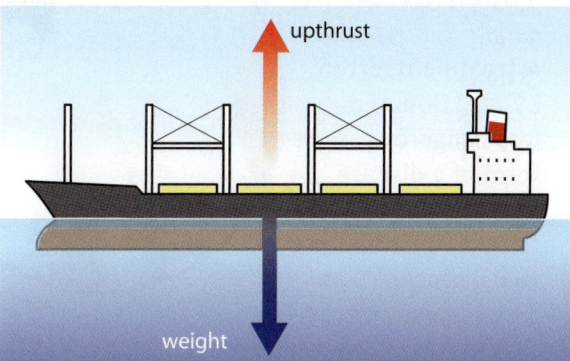

upthrust *noun*   قوة الدفع المؤثرة

The upward force on an object when it is immersed in fluid

The *upthrust* is equal to the weight of the fluid displaced (pushed aside).

The *upthrust* on a floating object exactly balances its weight.

UV *noun*   (الأشعة) فوق البنفسجية

Ultraviolet radiation – invisible rays that travel in the same way as light

Too much exposure to *UV* radiation from the Sun can damage your eyes and skin.

The hole in the ozone layer allows more *UV* radiation to reach the Earth's surface.

a b c d e f g h i j k l m n o p q r s t **u** v w x y z

Vv

vaccination
noun   تطعيم

A treatment, often by injection of a less dangerous form of a disease, that allows the body to build up immunity to a disease

Edward Jenner discovered that the disease smallpox could be prevented by **vaccination** with cowpox.

Vaccination programmes help prevent epidemics of diseases such as measles and tuberculosis.

vacuum   *noun*   خواء / فراغ

Empty space that contains no matter, not even air

Sounds cannot travel through a *vacuum*.
Light and heat radiation travel through the *vacuum* of space to reach the Earth.

variable   *noun*   متغيّر

A factor or condition that can take different values

The important *variables* in this investigation are the thickness of the sample and the temperature.

In a fair test, all *variables*, apart from the one you are investigating, are kept the same.

vector   *noun*   ناقل

An animal that carries the cause of a disease from one host to another

Mosquitoes are the **vectors** for the transmission of malaria between humans. In Africa, the tsetse fly is a **vector** for sleeping sickness.

vein   *noun*   وريد/عِرق

A blood vessel that returns blood from the body to the heart; also a fine tube in a leaf that transports water and nutrients

Blood in a **vein** contains less oxygen than blood in an artery.

The pattern of the **veins** in a leaf can help you identify the tree.

vertebrate
noun   فقاري

An animal with a backbone

There are five groups of **vertebrates**: mammals, birds, reptiles, amphibians and fish.

Vertebrates have an internal skeleton made from bone.

vibration   *noun*   اهتزاز

Rapid to and fro movement

Vibration creates sound waves that travel through the air.

The *vibration* of a guitar string is so fast that it appears as a blur.

a b c d e f g h i j k l m n o p q r s t u v w x y z

volume

virtual *adjective* تخيلي/افتراضي
Describes something that appears like a real object, but is not really there
Your image in a mirror is *virtual* – it is not really behind the mirror surface.
A *virtual* image cannot be projected onto a screen.

virus *noun* فيروس

A tiny infectious particle that may cause disease
A *virus* is smaller than a bacterium.
Scientists do not class a *virus* as a living thing because it cannot reproduce independently; to reproduce, a *virus* must infect a cell.

vitamin *noun* فيتامين
An essential substance that we require in small quantities for health
Fresh fruit and vegetables are good sources of *vitamins*.
Scurvy is a disease caused by a deficiency of *vitamin* C in the diet.

viviparous *adjective* ولود
Describes an animal that gives birth to live young
Almost all mammals are *viviparous*.
Some snakes are *viviparous*; their eggs hatch inside the mother's body, and then the young are born.

volcano *noun* بركان
A break in the Earth's surface, through which melted rock and hot gases rise
Lava may build up around a *volcano* to form a cone-shaped mountain.
It is difficult to predict exactly when a *volcano* will erupt.

volt (V) *noun* فولت
A unit that measures how much electrical energy a power source gives to electric charge
The torch uses two 1.5-*volt* batteries connected in series.
A 240-*volt* supply can give you a lethal shock.

volume
noun حجم
The amount of space something fills
A cube with 1 cm sides has a *volume* of 1 cubic centimetre (1 cm^3).
Calculate the *volume* of the room by multiplying its length by its breadth by its height.

$1 m^3 = 1 m \times 1 m \times 1 m$
1 m
1 m 1 m

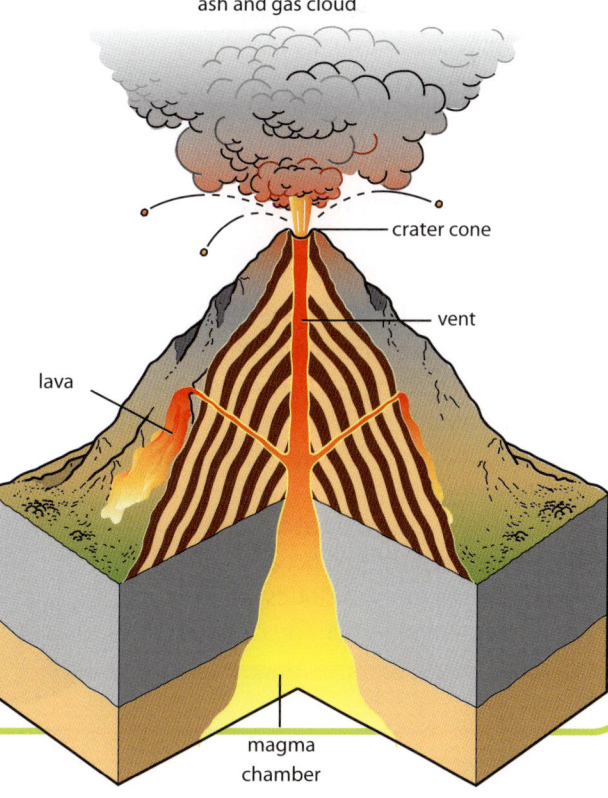
ash and gas cloud
crater cone
vent
lava
magma chamber

a b c d e f g h i j k l m n o p q r s t u v **w** x y z

Ww

weight *noun* وزن

The measure of how heavy something is; the force that pulls an object to the ground

An object's *weight* is created by the force of gravity acting on it. Because *weight* is a force it is measured in newtons.

waste *noun* فضلات / نفايات / فاقد

Unwanted, leftover materials

We should dispose of domestic *waste* in ways that minimise harm to the environment.

Living things excrete *waste* products produced by their cells.

water *noun* الماء

The most common liquid on Earth

Water is a compound of hydrogen and oxygen with the formula H_2O.

Water is the only substance that can be found as a solid (ice), a liquid and a gas (water vapour) on Earth.

water cycle

noun دورة الماء

The process by which water circulates through living and non-living things in the environment

The *water cycle* is powered by heat from the Sun.

In the *water cycle*, water evaporates from the oceans, condenses to form clouds and falls to the ground as rain (precipitation).

weightless

adjective عديم الوزن

Without weight

Astronauts in space experience *weightless* conditions.

When you are *weightless* there is no sense of up or down.

wetland *noun* أرض رطبة

An ecosystem such as a swamp or marsh where the soil is constantly wet

Many beautiful bird species can be seen in *wetland* habitats.

Wetland ecosystems are easily damaged by pollution.

year

wind *noun*   رياح
The movement of air in the atmosphere
The force of the *wind* can lift kites and turn mills.
The Khamsin is a hot *wind* that blows from the desert.

wind energy *noun*   طاقة الرياح
The use of wind as an energy source
Wind energy is a renewable energy source.
A wind turbine transforms *wind energy* into electricity.

wind speed *noun*   سرعة الرياح
The rate at which the wind blows (how fast it blows); the wind's strength
An anemometer is a weather instrument for recording *wind speed*.
In a hurricane, the *wind speed* is greater than 119 km/h.

worm *noun*   دودة
An invertebrate animal without legs and with a thin, soft body
Worms in the soil are decomposers.
Some *worms* are parasites; they may infect the human gut.

Yy

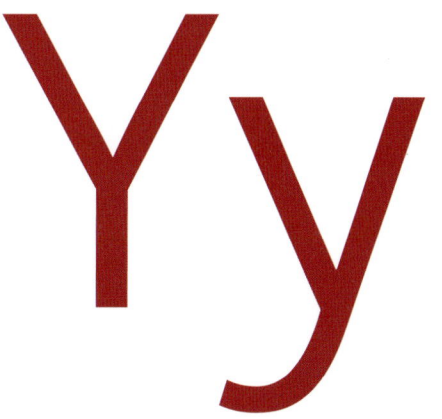

year *noun*   عام / سنة
The time taken for the Earth to complete one orbit of the Sun
In astronomy, 1 *year* lasts 365.25 days.
A normal calendar *year* is 365 days. A leap year (every fourth *year*) is 366 days.